3/03

39.95

Events That Changed
America Through the
Seventeenth Century

Events That Changed America Through the Seventeenth Century

Edited by
John E. Findling
&
Frank W. Thackeray

THE GREENWOOD PRESS
"EVENTS THAT CHANGED AMERICA" SERIES

GREENWOOD PRESS
Westport, Connecticut • London

Library of Congress Cataloging-in-Publication Data

Events that changed America through the seventeenth century / edited by John E.
Findling and Frank W. Thackeray.
    p. cm.—(The Greenwood Press "Events that changed America" series)
    Includes bibliographical references and index.
    ISBN 0–313–29083–0
    1. America—History—To 1810. 2. United States—History—Colonial period, ca.
1600–1775. I. Findling, John E. II. Thackeray, Frank W. III. Series.
E18.82.E94 2000
973.2—dc21   00–020080

British Library Cataloguing in Publication Data is available.

Library of Congress Catalog Card Number: 00–020080
ISBN: 0–313–29083–0

First published in 2000

Greenwood Press, 88 Post Road West, Westport, CT 06881
An imprint of Greenwood Publishing Group, Inc.
www.greenwood.com

Printed in the United States of America

The paper used in this book complies with the
Permanent Paper Standard issued by the National
Information Standards Organization (Z39.48–1984).

10 9 8 7 6 5 4 3 2 1

Contents

Illustrations

Preface

This volume, which describes and evaluates the significance of ten of the most important events in America prior to the eighteenth century, is the fourth in a multivolume series intended to acquaint readers with the seminal events of American history. Earlier volumes, published between 1996 and 1998, highlighted events in the eighteenth, nineteenth, and twentieth centuries, and this volume completes the series. There is also an ongoing series of volumes addressing the global experience. In addition, a new series will focus on events that changed Great Britain.

Our collective classroom experience provided the inspiration for this project. Having encountered literally thousands of students whose knowledge of the history of their country was sadly deficient, we determined to prepare a series of books that would concentrate on the most important events affecting those students (and others as well) in the hope that they would better understand their country and how it came to be. Furthermore, we hope these books will stimulate the reader to delve further into the events covered in each volume and to take a greater interest in history in general.

The current volume is designed to serve two purposes. First, the editors have provided an introduction that presents factual material about each event in a clear, concise, chronological order. Second, each introduction is followed by a longer interpretive essay by a specialist exploring the ramifications of the event under consideration. Each essay concludes with an annotated bibliography of the most important works about the event. The ten chapters are followed by two appendixes that provide additional information useful to the reader. Appendix A is a glossary of names, events, organizations, and terms mentioned but not fully explained in the introductions and interpretive essays. Appendix B is a timeline of key events corresponding to the time period this book covers. One editorial note: the spellings of the names of Indian tribes and individual Indians often varies among authorities. For example, one can spell the name of a New England tribe, the Nipmucs, Nipmucks, Nipmets, and Neepmucks. We have attempted to employ the spelling used by the most recent and authoritative sources (which do not always agree among themselves!), including Frederick Hoxie, ed., *Encyclopedia of North American Indians*, Boston: Houghton Mifflin, 1996; Carl Waldman, *Encyclopedia of Native American Tribes*, New York: Facts On File, 1988; and Judith Nies, *Native American History*, New York: Ballantine Books, 1996.

The events covered in this volume were selected on the basis of our combined teaching and research activities. Of course, another pair of editors might have arrived at a somewhat different list than we did, but we believe that we have assembled a group of events that truly changed America before the eighteenth century.

As with all published works, numerous people behind the scenes deserve much of the credit for the final product. Barbara Rader, our editor at Greenwood Press, has encouraged us from the very beginning. The staff of the photographic division of the Library of Congress provided genial assistance to us as we selected the photographs that appear in this book. We are especially grateful to Brigette Colligan who was always ready to type or retype whatever we asked her to. Special thanks go to Lindsay Pritchett whose student essay on the Salem witch trials formed the basis for the introduction to that chapter in the book, and to Carol Findling who reshaped the essay for publication. Thanks too to the friendly people who work for the library and the Division of Humanities at Macquarie University in Sydney, Australia, and the Stout Research Centre at Victoria University in Wellington, New Zealand, where this book was finished during a sabbatical leave. We benefited from funds that Indiana University Southeast provided for student research assistants and for other costs associated with the project.

We are grateful to Roger and Amy Baylor and Kate O'Connell for making their establishment available to us, enabling us to confer about the project and discuss its many facets with our colleagues and former students in a congenial atmosphere. Among those who helped us in one way or another to make this a better book are John Newman, Sheila Andersen, Sam Sloss, Kim Pelle, and Glenn Crothers. And, most importantly, we thank our authors, whose essays were well conceived and thoughtful and whose patience when the project seemed to lag was much appreciated.

Finally, we wish to express our appreciation to our spouses, Carol Findling and Kathy Thackeray, and to our aging children, Jamey and Jenny Findling and Alex and Max Thackeray, whose support and interest in our work made it all worthwhile.

John E. Findling
Frank W. Thackeray

This photograph shows a twentieth-century replica of Columbus's flagship, the *Santa Maria*. (Reproduced from the Collections of the Library of Congress.)

1

First Encounters, c. 40,000 B.C.E.–1492 C.E.

INTRODUCTION

Scholars generally agree that human beings first came to what is now the United States from northeastern Asia, crossing overland at the point of the present-day Bering Sea. During this time, which archaeologists believe was between forty to seventy thousand years ago, the Ice Age had lowered ocean levels to the point where a wide stretch of land connected Asia with North America, creating a land geographers refer to as Beringia. Groups of nomadic people, searching for game or vegetation for sustenance, moved through Beringia into Alaska.

Later, as the glaciers retreated, Beringia fell below sea level and Asia and North America were separated. Those left in Alaska became North America's first indigenous people. Scholars do not agree on just when significant migrations into the more southern parts of North America took place, but all agree that people moved into the southern parts of North America at least nineteen thousand years ago and into South America at least thirteen thousand years ago.

The earliest indigenous peoples of North America were hunters and gatherers, killing bison, bear, deer, elk, and other game with increasingly sophisticated spear points and supplementing their diets with fish and berries. Archaeological evidence suggests that after 6000 B.C.E., many Native people, while still hunters and gatherers, began living in larger houses and communities, making pottery, and adapting more creatively to their environment. Sometime after 5000 B.C.E., plant cultivation began in Mexico and spread northward unevenly, depending on the terrain and weather conditions. Corn, beans, gourds, and squash were among the first crops to be planted, although in some places this did not occur until 1000 B.C.E. At that point, the fundamental features of Native American culture were in place, and the years toward 1492 saw these cultures growing in social complexity and population.

Scholars disagree on the pre-1492 population of the Americas. Until the 1950s, the figures of 8 million for the entire Western Hemisphere and 1 million for North America were generally accepted, but more recent analyses of the available evidence suggest a much larger population. Many scholars now estimate that between 75 and 145 million people inhabited the Western Hemisphere in 1492, of whom between 12 and 18 million lived in North America. There may well have been more people living in the Americas at this time than lived in Europe and Russia combined.

For thousands of years there was no contact whatsoever between Europe and the Americas. While Christopher Columbus is acknowledged to have been the first European to establish permanent settlements in the hemisphere, he was by no means the first visitor there. Legends and accounts from various northern European cultures, combined with archaeological evidence found in North America, inform us that Europeans knew of North America hundreds of years before Columbus set sail.

In the mid-sixth century, according to legend, a Irish monk known as St. Brendan (b. 489) took a long voyage and ended up in a magical place called the Land of Promise, where all the plants were in constant bloom, all the trees had delicious fruit, and all the stones were gems. Some other passages in the account suggest that St. Brendan sailed across the northern Atlantic, but no one seriously believes that St. Brendan or other Irish explorers after him ever got past Iceland.

The pagan Norse people began depredations in England in 793 and probably had established colonies in Iceland by 800. By 980, the Norse had settled Greenland's southeastern coast, just 500 miles from Labrador in northeastern Canada. Around the year 1000, Leif Eriksson made landfall on Baffin Island, north of Labrador, on Labrador itself, and at another land that he called Vinland, probably the northern peninsula of present-day Newfoundland. Eriksson's exploits led to four more voyages to Vinland shortly after this, and sporadic voyages and short-lived settlements for perhaps another 300 years after that. Norse accounts of these voyages are supported by scattered archaeological findings, but scholars still know very little about the extent and duration of these settlements. The Norse were never plentiful enough nor well-armed enough to forge a permanent colony in the midst of what was, even then, a significant Native American population.

Another legendary pre-Columbian settler was Madoc, a Welsh prince who, some believe, came to America in the twelfth century and founded a number of colonies in locations as diverse as Newfoundland and Mexico. The Yarmouth Stone, a rock with mysterious inscriptions discovered in Nova Scotia, and the Newport Tower, a stone structure found in Rhode Island, have been advanced as evidence of Madoc's visits to America, but most scholars remain unconvinced. Others identify Madoc with Quetzalcoatl, a white man who in Aztec legend visited Mexico at about the same time Madoc is supposed to have come to America.

There is, however, credible evidence that ships were traveling from Norway to Iceland and Greenland fairly regularly by the fourteenth century, but if these vessels sailed any closer to the eastern shore of the Canadian arctic, they were just passing by and their crews made no effort to establish settlements. These contacts with Canada increased during the fifteenth century, and at the end of that century, an Italian, Giovanni Caboto, better known as John Cabot, was probably the first European to sail along the coast of eastern North America and recognize it for what it was.

Although most of the pre-Columbian contacts with America had been with Canada, the first permanent European settlements were well to the south, in the islands of the Caribbean. This is where Christopher Columbus and the many Europeans who followed him first encountered the indigenous peoples of America with such devastating effects.

Born in 1451 in Genoa, an Italian port city, Columbus had only a rudimentary education and as a boy and a young man, worked at several trades, including weaving. From an early age, however, he was fascinated by the sea and began working on Mediterranean merchant ships while still in his teens. In the mid-1470s, he went to Lisbon, Portugal, where he took advantage of the maritime economy to become a much better sailor. In Lisbon, he learned much about earlier voyages and the search for a western route to Asia, and he married into a well-connected Portuguese family.

In 1485, when the Portuguese king would not sanction and support Columbus's plan for a voyage to find Asia by going west, Columbus went to Spain. By this time, Spain had been united by the marriage of Ferdinand and Isabella, and Columbus began seeking support for a voyage as early as 1486. At this time, however, Spain was fighting the Moorish stronghold of Granada, and Columbus's supplications were not approved until early 1492, and then only to keep him from going elsewhere.

In all, Columbus made four voyages to what came to be known as the New World. His first voyage, 1492–93, took him to the Bahamas, Cuba, and Hispaniola (the island where Haiti and the Dominican Republic are located). On his second voyage, 1493–96, he visited Guadeloupe, the Leeward Islands, the Virgin Islands, and Puerto Rico. His third voyage, 1498–1500, took him along the northeast coast of South America, to Trinidad and then to the established colony on Hispaniola. There he got into political trouble and was sent back to Spain a prisoner in chains. He regained royal favor and made a fourth and final visit, 1502–4, sailing along the coast of Central America from Honduras to Panama and stopping at other Caribbean islands.

In recent years and especially during 1992, the observance of the quincentenary of Columbus's first voyage, scholars have fiercely attacked the reputations of Columbus and other early European explorers and colonizers in America. As the interpretive essay points out, the Europeans treated the indigenous peoples they encountered with great brutality as they attempted to enslave them, plunder their valuables, or simply exterminate them. Perhaps the epidemic diseases the Europeans brought with them to America killed even more Indians than did the guns and swords of the colonizers.

Epidemic diseases, mostly smallpox, measles, and influenza, first began killing Amerindians (the name given to Indians living in the Caribbean at the time of the first encounters with Europeans) in 1493 with the arrival of the ships of Columbus's second voyage. Smallpox was especially deadly among the Indians on the various Caribbean islands, because they had no natural immunity to this strange new disease, and an epidemic in 1518 attracted much commentary among Spanish colonial writers.

Measles was first reported in force during the 1530s, when an African slave could have spread it. Known in Europe, measles did not kill many whites, as smallpox sometimes did, but 25 or 30 percent of the Indians who caught it died, a figure that remained constant throughout the colonial period. The sixteenth century is marked with a series of deadly epidemics, notably in the 1540s, the late 1550s, and between 1576 and

1591. By the end of the century, typhus, mumps, and possibly bubonic plague had been added to the list of fatal diseases. Some scholars estimate that more than 90 percent of the Indians in the Americas died from European-introduced diseases.

INTERPRETIVE ESSAY
Andrew Frank

"In fourteen hundred and ninety-two, Columbus sailed the ocean blue . . ." Across the nation, countless schoolteachers annually recite these lines to commemorate the trans-Atlantic travels of Christopher Columbus and his "discovery" of the "New World" in October 1492. Indeed, American history often begins with a discussion of the Italian-born sailor, his financing from Spain's King Ferdinand and Queen Isabella, and his three ships, the *Niña*, *Pinta*, and *Santa María*. Columbus Day is currently celebrated as a national holiday in the United States, and most Americans believe that this journey to the New World initiated American history. Despite the poem that is often recited and the holiday celebrated in his name, Americans often miss the grand importance of Columbus's arrival in the New World. Rather than a beginning, the year 1492 marked a revolutionary turning point in world and American history.

The New World that Columbus and subsequent European explorers encountered was neither unsettled nor in need of discovery. For that matter, it was not even "new." Instead, the first human settlers migrated to North America twelve to forty thousand years before Columbus made his more famous journey. Rather than sailing across the Atlantic Ocean in three caravels, these small bands of early migrants crossed a land bridge that covered what is now the Bering Strait, a narrow stretch of water and ice that separates eastern Siberia from the western coast of Alaska. During the Ice Age, falling temperatures caused glaciers to grow and ocean levels to drop. This process exposed a stretch of land as wide as one thousand miles. Scientists call this region, which now lies some 120 feet under water, Beringia. Bands of nomadic Asian hunters, consisting of approximately twenty-five people each, gradually crossed Beringia as they searched for and followed large game animals—especially the mammoth. These migrations brought an unknown number of nomadic hunters, or Paleo-Indians, deeper and deeper into the Americas.

There, on lands previously uninhabited by humans, they found new hunting territories, rich natural resources, and hospitable climates. When the ice melted and the ocean waters separated the continents once again, the migration ended. This trapped an unknown number of bands in the Americas. By 10,000 B.C.E., descendants of these migrants had settled almost all of North and South America.

Over the course of thousands of years, the Paleo-Indians adapted to their diverse surroundings and formed countless communities across the Americas. Almost all of these communities used kinship or family groups, often called clans, to determine social, economic, political, and religious obligations. Despite their common ancestry, each of these tribes eventually developed its own thriving and distinct culture. The Indians spoke hundreds of languages, used various tools, and often traced themselves back to different ancestors. Some lived in agrarian societies while others hunted and gathered; some lived in permanent cities and villages while others lived more nomadic lives. Pre-Columbian Indians fought wars with each other, traded goods with one another, and created specialized crafts and elaborate pieces of art. Columbus and his men stumbled upon a world thousands of years old, and whose peoples had established cultures rich in heritage and history.

In every region of the Americas, Indians had distinct cultures and lifestyles. In New England, for example, the region was filled with small Algonquian villages that normally contained fewer than 300 residents. These hunter-gatherers were divided into hundreds of tribes: among them the Abenakis, Mohegans, Wampanoags, Narragansetts, Nipmucs, Pocumtucks, Mohawks, and Mashpees. Kin groups in each of these small tribes followed a seasonal pattern of hunting, fishing, shellfish collecting, plant gathering, and small-scale agriculture. Coastal bands harvested salmon, shad, eel, sturgeon, and whale. Indians farther inland hunted moose, deer, black bear, and beaver. Rather than following hereditary chiefs, these Algonquians made political decisions by consensus and gave authority to those who could lead and persuade others to agree. Quite a different Indian culture emerged in what is now California. There, pre-Columbian Indians grew tobacco and harvested dozens of other foods that grew naturally in the area. The men hunted and fished, and the women prepared these foodstuffs for consumption and storage. These Indians typically lived in villages that numbered around one thousand. Native peoples lived in even larger groups in what is today Florida. There, Indians lived in chiefdoms that numbered in the thousands. In these hierarchical societies, most villages paid tribute to the larger and more powerful chiefdoms. Most Indian men hunted while women spent much of their time cultivating crops. Some of Florida's Indians used slash and burn techniques to ensure plentiful crops, and nearly all of the Indian communities in the southeast grew the "holy trinity" of corn, beans, and squash. The emphasis on agriculture allowed many Indians in Florida to work as specialized artisans, full-time soldiers, or bureaucrats. In sum, pre-Columbian Indians did not share a single lifestyle.

Diversity also characterized the religions practiced by Indians in pre-Columbian America. Some Native Americans believed that spirits of gods inhabited the trees around them; others believed that they lived in a cosmic drama in which the gods competed for power. Some, like the northeastern Iroquois, believed that their ancestors fell from the sky, while others, like the southwestern Navajo, believed that their ancestors emerged from the earth. The religious ceremonies and rituals of these diverse peoples involved altars and sacrifices, dances and songs, chants and potions. Many of these events took place on a seasonal calendar, especially those that celebrated the harvest, like the Cherokee's Green Corn Ceremony. Other ceremonies, like the Plains Indians' Sun Dance, were less tied to the calendar.

Estimates of the Native American population in 1492 vary widely for good reasons: no census was taken by Native peoples before the arrival of Europeans; archeological findings conflict with each other, are incomplete, or are difficult to assess; and European observers only wrote about the handful of peoples that they encountered in the decades after contact. Limited sources, as well as ethnocentric attitudes about Indians' culture that guided early scholarship, led most early twentieth-century scholars to underestimate the Indian population on the eve of European contact. Until rather recently, most scholars believed that no more than one million Native Americans lived north of Mexico in 1492. In essence, they believed that the land that later became the United States was a "virgin land" untouched by human hands before the arrival of Europeans. In recent years, this description has been radically reassessed. The Smithsonian Institution, perhaps the most conservative participant in the debate, has doubled its estimate, claiming that there "may have been as many as two million" inhabitants in the region. Most recent scholars have offered more revolutionary reassessments of pre-Columbian America. Rather than being an empty or underpopulated continent, these demographers have convincingly shown that before the arrival of Europeans at least twelve to eighteen million Indians made their homes in what is now the United States. In North and South America, the Native American population probably ranged between 43 and 65 million. Other scholars have asserted that the population for the Americas may have even approached 100 million or as much as one-fifth of the Earth's human population. Scholars have not reached consensus in demographic assessments of pre-Columbian America. This debate over numbers promises to continue, but the idea of the Americas as empty land has been universally dismissed. Scholars, even as they disagree over actual numbers, now agree that much of America was well populated by 1492.

Rather than "virgin" soil, the Americas became what historian Francis Jennings describes as "widowed land." America seemed empty to sixteenth-, seventeenth-, and eighteenth-century Europeans because most of its inhabitants had died. In the decades following contact, nearly all Native communities lost at least half of their population, and most communities suffered from even higher mortality rates. In the century after European contact, America's total Indian population dropped between 90 and 95 percent. This widespread depopulation began as a result of the arrival of Columbus and other European explorers and settlers. These European newcomers introduced a wide range of pathogens, flora, and fauna to American ecosystems in which they had never before existed. This Columbian exchange—the most important ramification of Columbus's journey—transferred countless pathogens, grains, grasses, large mammals, small rodents, insects, trees, shrubs, and birds. The introduction of European diseases to the Americas resulted in the rapid depopulation of Native populations. The arrival of American grains across the Atlantic fed a surging European population. New technology transformed Native society, and the introduction of sugar cane to the Americas was soon followed by the arrival of African slaves. In short, the disruption caused by this biological exchange between the continents irrevocably altered the lives of Native Americans and humanity at large.

Before most Native Americans actually met a European explorer or colonist or heard of their existence, they felt the impact of the Columbian exchange's deadly pathogens. Germs, viruses, and bacteria entered a world that they had not been in before. The lack of exposure to these European diseases left Native peoples without biological immunity, genetic resistance, or effective medical responses to the new pathogens. Indians suffered disproportionately when diseases hit their communities for the first time. As a result, smallpox, measles, influenza, chicken pox, whooping cough, malaria, amoebic dysentery, diphtheria, and the bubonic plague killed all or nearly all of the inhabitants of some Indian villages. After traveling in New Netherland in 1656, for example, Dutchman Adriaen Van der Donck wrote that "the Indians . . . affirm, that before the arrival of the Christians, and before the small pox broke out amongst them, they were ten times as numerous as they now are, and that their population had been melted down by this disease, whereof nine-tenths of them have died." Even though Columbus and other early explorers did not venture far from the Atlantic Coast, Native nations that lived as far west as California confronted the full force of the European diseases that spread across the Americas.

Those who survived the initial onslaught of the European diseases faced the nightmare of dealing with the sick, infirm, and the deceased. After the loss of young adults to death and sickness, Indian villages could not meet their nutritional needs through hunting and farming. Throughout the Americas, the ensuing starvation and malnutrition simply added to the mounting death tolls. In the early seventeenth century, Governor William Bradford found coastal New England to be nearly barren, the Indians "being dead & abundantly wasted in the last great mortality which fell in these parts about three years before the coming of the English, wherein thousands of them dyed." Bradford was further struck by the Indians "not being able to burie one another; their sculs and bones were found in many places lying still above ground, where their houses & dwellings had been."

The epidemics haunted Native Americans long after the initial contacts with European pathogens. Although Native Americans slowly built immunities to the new diseases, smallpox, measles, bubonic plague, and influenza continued to cripple the Native communities into the eighteenth and nineteenth centuries. Some Guale, Timucua, and Apalachee Indians, for example, survived the waves of disease that ravaged the southeast in the sixteenth and seventeenth centuries, but newer epidemics had wiped them out by the American Revolution. Similarly, in 1763, Ottawa Indians suffered from smallpox after Lord Jeffrey Amherst gave them blankets that previously had been used to cover infected British soldiers. The disease quickly spread among the Delaware, Mingo, Miami, and several other Indian nations. Some one hundred thousand Indians lost their lives in this epidemic. Fatal disease, along with falling birth rates, increased warfare, and famine prevented Indian populations from returning to their previous numbers. The disruption of the Columbian exchange clearly outlived Columbus.

The widespread destruction of Native peoples caused a restructuring of tribal and national affiliations across the Americas. The creation of the Creek Confederacy in what later became Georgia and Florida typified this process. When Hernando de Soto plundered through the southeast in 1540 looking for gold, he encountered dozens of individual Indian chiefdoms, including the Coosa, Apalachee, and the Alabama. There was no Creek Confederacy. The deadly European diseases that de Soto's Spanish forces left behind, however, resulted in the collapse in the region's Native population. Over the next century, the survivors regrouped and formed a new entity that eventually became known as the Creek Confederacy. Ethnic Muskogee Indians, later known as the Creeks, were at the core of this new polity. To bolster their size and strength, the Muskogees invited the remnants of other southeastern Indian nations and villages into their confederation. By the eighteenth century, thousands of non-Muskogee Indians from dozens of ethnic groups had made a home among the ever-expanding Confederacy. For this reason, the Creeks were the only Indian group to see its population expand in the seventeenth and eighteenth centuries.

Declining populations led to tribal restructuring throughout the Americas during the sixteenth and seventeenth centuries. For example, in New England, Indians who had earlier lived in small bands became dependent on the fur trade with French and English traders. This encouraged the region's small bands to create mechanisms of centralized power, or a single chief, to negotiate with the Europeans who were hesitant to deal with countless leaders. Political restructuring also altered the Iroquois Confederacy. This Native alliance, also known as the Iroquois League or Five Nations, existed before the arrival of Europeans. Even so, the arrival of Europeans and Old World pathogens created new demands. By the 1680s, for the first time, village headmen from across the Iroquois League began consulting each other on a regular basis, and the Iroquois began speaking as a unified voice for the first time. In large part, this break from traditional forms of local authority resulted from the death of many prominent elders. As a group of Mohawk warriors asserted in 1691, "All those . . . who had sense are dead." The diseases of the Columbian exchange had taken their toll.

The Columbian exchange brought more than new diseases to the Americas. It also introduced new plants and animals that reshaped the American environment and Indian economies. After 1492, the flora and fauna of the Americas and Europe, whose plants and animals had existed isolated from one another, slowly became more alike. Indeed, the ecosystem of fifteenth-century America seemed to be radically different from the European scenery to which Columbus had become accustomed. Columbus wrote, "I saw neither sheep nor goats nor any other beast. . . .

If there were any I couldn't have failed to see them." Columbus did not encounter domesticated animals in his travels, and the animals that he did observe were often unlike anything he had seen before. Generations of European settlers and scientists confirmed these initial observations. The New World alligators and crocodiles startled the Europeans as the Old World had no reptiles larger than the iguana. Even stranger to European sensibilities were the electric eels and flesh-eating piranhas found in the Americas. The exotic American scenery also included monkeys that could swing from their tails, snakes with rattles on their tails, as well as huge bison and buffalo. The range of insects, the size of the rodents, and the plethora of freshwater fish similarly surprised the Europeans.

The arrival of European animals to the Americas transformed the American countryside. In addition to cattle and swine, Europeans also brought chickens, sheep, horses, and domesticated dogs and cats. Sometimes Europeans transplanted the new animals to fit their uniquely European needs. Members of the seventeenth-century Virginian gentry, for example, introduced red foxes to the Chesapeake region in order to participate in English-style hunting. Similarly, some Dutch and English settlers introduced honeybees to the Americas to provide an Old World sweetener to their diet. Other imports came as unintentional stowaways on the trans-Atlantic vessels that brought explorers and colonists. In this way, English sparrows filled the skies of colonial America, and the American cockroach, brought over on slave ships from Africa, infested colonial homes.

The European plants of the Columbian exchange further changed the American countryside. Soon after his arrival in the New World, Columbus observed that "all the trees were so different from ours as day from night, and so the fruits, the herbage, the rocks, and all things." Within decades, America contained much of what Columbus believed it lacked. Like the first wave of disease and some of the animals, much of the flora that came to the Americas accidentally took root in America. Colonists transported seeds for grasses and clovers unwittingly in the textiles, blankets, and dirty boots brought from Europe. In this way, Europeans unwittingly transformed much of the countryside. By 1700, for example, a European bluegrass covered Kentucky. Daisies and dandelions, not indigenous to the Americas, also spread across the countryside.

Many other plants made their way into the New World because of the conscious designs of explorers and settlers. Indeed, almost immediately after their arrival in the Americas, Europeans worked to change the New

World to fit their image of the Old World. Spanish friars, for example, introduced wheat to grow the grain needed to make communion wafers. Europeans also imported and planted chickpeas, melons, onions, radishes, grapes, olives, and bananas. These crops changed the landscape and helped dictate the path that colonization would take. Perhaps most important to the development of the early colonies, European settlers introduced sugar cane in the Caribbean and South America. The ramifications of this import were felt worldwide as Europeans turned to African slaves to tend to the highly profitable crop. In the centuries that followed, slave traders brought at least eleven million enslaved Africans to the Americas to cultivate this and other labor-intensive crops.

The incorporation of new animals in Native societies was not necessarily a smooth process. On one hand, many Indian people took advantage of the new animals. Plains Indians, such as the Comanche and Cheyenne, used horses to hunt buffalo and other large game. Navajo and Pueblo Indians incorporated sheep and goats into their diet and economy. Cherokee, Creek, and Choctaw Indians domesticated cattle. At the same time, however, the arrival of some new animals disrupted many traditional patterns. Newly introduced range animals competed with indigenous game for scarce grazing grounds and water supplies and also trampled over Indian cornfields. At times, disputes over animals resulted in warfare. Southeastern Indians, even as they incorporated domesticated animals into their diet, constantly complained to the colonial governments of Georgia and South Carolina about the damage done by the free-range pigs and cattle that the English had introduced. Similarly, in seventeenth-century New England, many Indians incorporated domesticated pigs into their lifestyles. The ensuing disputes over grazing rights resulted in many small skirmishes that contributed to the outbreak of King Philip's War in 1675–76.

The Columbian exchange also brought new technology and products to the New World. These products, which included metal tools, guns, and liquor, reshaped the lifestyle of the Native Americans. Most Indians quickly replaced tools made of bone and wood with metallic versions. Europeans traders offered steel axes and knives, iron kettles, woolen clothing, blankets, linen shirts, jackets, scissors, thimbles, needles and thread in return for valuable animal pelts, furs, and skins. The demand for European items created networks of trade between European and Indian communities. In many Native communities, the demands for European goods resulted in the increased "production" of animal furs. With men spending more time hunting and women spending more time preparing pelts for trade, Indian peoples became increasingly dependent on Europeans for food and clothing. This dependence often resulted in greater demands by European traders, increased prices for trade goods, new political loyalties, and occasionally the sale of tribal lands to pay off mounting debts. At times, Indians sold their enemies to European slave traders in return for desired trade goods.

The Indian trade often resulted in the entrance of European settlers into Indian villages. Thousands of intermarriages between Indian women and European men occurred in colonial America, especially in the Great Lakes region and the lower southeast. Native wives proved to be invaluable assets to European traders because they provided companionship and residences, solicited business, and informed them about the community's general temperature. Furthermore, traders benefited from the labor of their wives who interpreted for them, collected debts from Indians, prepared animal skins for market, and as British traveler John Lawson explained, "instruct[ed] [th]em in the Affairs and Customs of the Country."

Intermarriages in the lower south, especially within the Creek, Cherokee, and Choctaw Nations, created generations of "mixed" individuals. Often these so-called half breeds became proponents of acculturation. They helped bring African slaves, cotton cultivation, centralized forms of government, and written laws to Native society. By the early nineteenth century, the Cherokees had a tribal government that reflected European systems. The new tribal government contained a bicameral legislature, elected officials, an elected head chief with a limited term of power, and a court system.

Among the new ideas that Europeans brought to the New World, perhaps the most intrusive was Christianity. Few Europeans saw anything in Indian society that they recognized as organized religion. At best, they saw Indians as unchurched individuals immersed in superstition; at worst, they believed Indians practiced devil worship. In either case, Europeans viewed Indians as prime candidates for "the work tending to the enlargement of the Kingdom of Jesus Christ." European missionaries attempted to convert Indians throughout North and South America. In almost every case, Indian peoples saw these attempts as hostile assaults on their traditional beliefs and customs.

Only a handful of seventeenth-century Christian missionaries successfully converted many Indian peoples in what later became the United States. Puritan ministers, led by John Eliot, established "praying towns" for the conversion of New England's Wampanoag Indians in 1646. The most successful of these missions was established at Martha's Vineyard where 282 Indians entered the covenant and an Indian church was established. The Massachusetts Bay Company used the power of the law to coerce neighboring Indians into converting, but even this could not convince most of the New England's Natives to accept Christianity. By the end of the seventeenth century only four of the original "praying towns" remained. Farther south, Spain established over 150 missions in Florida. Spanish friars obtained the allegiance of thousands of Guale, Timucua, and Apalachee Indians and extracted the labor of their parishioners. Most of these missions were short lived, however, and by 1700 there were no remaining Guale or Timucua converts. Within a few decades, Spain had to abandon nearly all of its missions among the Apalachee Indians.

Apart from these short-lived successes, most Christian missionaries had difficulty converting Indian peoples. This frustrated many religious leaders who, instead of looking at the intrusive behavior of the Christian missionaries, found fault in the "Indian's character." Methodist leader John Wesley, for example, believed that the Indians "insatiate love of drink, as well as other European vices" made conversion an impossible task. The Indians, he stated, "show no inclination to learn anything, but least of all Christianity." Indeed, as many Europeans noticed, so-called converted Indians never fully accepted Christianity on the missionaries' terms. In most cases, Indians blended Christian doctrines with their traditional beliefs and formed new syncretic faiths. British commissioner George Cartwright observed that in New England, "those whom they say are converted cannot be distinguished by their lives, manners, or habits from those who are not."

While Indian peoples suffered massive depopulation and cultural disruption, the Columbian exchange helped Europe's population to flourish. The Americas provided an endless list of new food including maize (or corn), several kinds of beans, potatoes, sweet potatoes, peanuts, tomatoes, pumpkins, papaya, squash, guava, avocados, pineapples, chili peppers, and cocoa beans. These agricultural products eventually turned the Americas into the breadbox of the world and allowed European farmers to increase their ability to feed themselves. These food products helped to put an end to the famine and fear of famine that had kept European populations in relative check in previous centuries. Europe, whose population hovered slightly above 100 million from 1450 to 1650, saw its population explode to 144 million in 1740 and 192 million in 1800. The introduction of American vegetables also affected the traditional foods of European cultures. Ireland adopted the potato as its central caloric source by the eighteenth century. Similarly, generations after it arrived in Europe, the tomato transformed Italian cuisine. Some nonedible crops transformed Europe as well. The Americas provided the world with tobacco, rubber, and most forms of cotton. These exports remained among the most lucrative for American farmers. Just as fortunate to the development of Europe, America did not export a deadly range of pathogens. Although some suggest that syphilis may have been transported to Europe from the Americas, there were no New World counterparts to smallpox, measles, or the bubonic plague. In comparison to the Americas where Native peoples primarily suffered from the Columbian exchange, Europeans generally prospered from the "new" American foods and raw materials.

In 1540, a mere five decades after the arrival of Columbus, a southeastern chief struggled to describe what the collision with the Old World meant to his people: "The things that seldom happen bring astonishment. Think, then, what must be the effect on me and mine, the sight of you and your people, whom we have at no time seen, stride the fierce brutes, your horses, entering with such speed and fury into my country, that we had not tidings of your coming." Astonishment, he admitted, hardly approached a description of what had happened after 1492 or of what impact the forces that Columbus's "discovery" unleashed. In the decades that preceded and followed this statement, Native societies witnessed waves of epidemics across the Americas, the alteration of their traditional diet and customs, a change in their trading and hunting patterns across the Americas, and a cultural assault on their religious belief systems by Christian missionaries. The Columbian exchange resulted in the population explosion of Europe and Asia, the massive population movement across the Atlantic, the rise of a trans-Atlantic slave trade, and the expansion of world trade. In short, Columbus may not have found a continent in need of "discovery," but he did make 1492 a turning point in world history.

SELECTED BIBLIOGRAPHY

Axtell, James. *Beyond 1492: Encounters in Colonial North America*. New York: Oxford University Press, 1992. A book of essays dealing with the first encounters between Europeans and Native Americans and the historical treatment of that event since 1492.
Bray, Warwick, et al. *The New World*. Oxford, England: Elsevier-Phaidon, 1975.

A heavily illustrated survey of the archeological and ethnological history of North America before 1492.

Cook, Noble David. *Born to Die: Disease and New World Conquest, 1492–1650*. Cambridge, England: Cambridge University Press, 1998. A survey of the various epidemics of smallpox, measles, typhus, and other diseases that proved fatal to millions of American Indians.

Denevan, William M., ed. *The Native Populations of the Americas in 1492*. 2nd ed. Madison: University of Wisconsin Press, 1992. First published in 1976 as a pioneer demographic study, this book has been updated and its conclusions altered based on more recent population studies.

Fernandez-Armesto, Filipe. *Columbus*. New York: Oxford University Press, 1992. Short, balanced account of the explorer's life and career.

Jennings, Francis. *The Invasion of America: Indians, Colonialism, and the Cant of Conquest*. Chapel Hill: University of North Carolina Press, 1975. Jennings was one of the first historians to look at European colonization from an Indian viewpoint.

Josephy, Alvin, M., Jr., ed. *America in 1492: The World of the Indian People Before the Arrival of Columbus*. New York: Knopf, 1992. A collection of scholarly articles on the various American Indian groups and their cultures in the fifteenth century.

———. *The Indian Heritage of America*. Rev. ed. Boston: Houghton-Mifflin, 1991. Josephy, a titan of American Indian history, devotes fully half of this survey history to the pre-conquest era.

Morison, Samuel Eliot. *Admiral of the Ocean Sea: A Life of Christopher Columbus*. Boston: Little, Brown, 1942. For many years this book stood as the definitive life of Columbus but is now outdated in its interpretation.

Oleson, Tryggvi J. *Early Voyages and Northern Approaches, 1000–1632*. Toronto: McClellan and Stewart, 1963. A history of the early voyages from Scandinavia and the British Isles to Iceland, Greenland, and North America.

Phillips, William D., Jr., and Carla Rahn Phillips. *The Worlds of Christopher Columbus*. Cambridge, England: Cambridge University Press, 1992. A study of Columbus and his times that treats him neither as a hero nor an unprincipled villain.

Stannard, David E. *American Holocaust: Columbus and the Conquest of the New World*. New York: Oxford University Press, 1992. A detailed history of the early encounters between Europeans and American Indians, with emphasis on the destructive effects of the diseases and purposeful violence that the Europeans brought.

Thornton, Russell. *American Indian Holocaust and Survival: A Population History Since 1492*. Norman: University of Oklahoma Press, 1987. A demographic study of the decline in Indian population from 1492 to 1900 and its rise since then.

2

The Expedition of Coronado, 1540–1542

INTRODUCTION

Coronado's expedition into the present-day southwest and south central United States was the most elaborate and far-reaching Spanish expedition into North America in the sixteenth century. But a number of other Spanish explorers paved the way for Coronado by sailing to the mainland of North America and spending months, sometimes years, trekking across unknown landscapes and sometimes enduring great hardships.

Juan Ponce de León arrived in the West Indies in 1508 and became governor of the island of San Juan (now Puerto Rico) in 1509. There he found some gold, and by 1512, he had amassed a considerable fortune. That year, King Ferdinand granted him permission to explore the islands to the north, in what is now the Bahamas. Natives from the north spoke of a spring that restored youth to those who drank from it. Such a spring was, however, unknown in the Bahamas, and the legend probably referred to limestone springs in Florida, which was then thought of as an island. But Ponce de León was far more interested in capturing slaves and enhancing his wealth than in spending his money seeking a fountain of youth. He left Puerto Rico in March 1513 and sailed northward through the Bahamas, reaching the St. Augustine area of Florida during

Coronado's expedition took him and his men through endless miles of barren countryside in the southwestern desert in search of fabulous treasure. (Reproduced from the Collections of the Library of Congress.)

Easter week or the Feast of Flowers, from which the place name is derived.

Turning south at that point, Ponce sailed back along the coast to the southern tip of Florida, then up the west coast to San Carlos Bay, where a skirmish with hostile Indians drove them back out to sea. The expedition returned to Puerto Rico in August 1513. In 1514 the king gave Ponce a contract to occupy and govern Florida, although he had found nothing of value there. Probably because of the slim prospect of finding wealth, Ponce did not return to Florida until 1521, when news of the great treasures being found in Mexico encouraged him to try again. His expedition made landfall in southwest Florida; there a fight with Indians resulted in a Spanish defeat and a fatal arrow wound for Ponce himself. His death, along with that of Francisco de Garay, another explorer who had died on a journey to the Gulf Coast, placed Spanish claims to the southeastern part of the United States in abeyance, waiting for the next, more successful expedition.

Garay had approached the Gulf Coast on his way to Mexico, where

Hernán Cortés was busy extending Spanish dominance on his own terms. After Cortés had reached Veracruz in 1519 on his way to plunder the Aztecs and assume control of Mexico, he broke ranks with Governor Diego Velásquez in Hispaniola. He had proclaimed himself de facto Spanish governor of Mexico, in effect seceding from Spanish colonial authority in the Caribbean and affirming his loyalty directly to the king.

Velásquez did not take this affront to his authority lightly and declared Cortés and his followers traitors. He authorized Garay to lead an expedition to displace Cortés, or at least limit the territory that the rebel was claiming, and offered Garay the governorship of the land north and east of Mexico as a reward. Garay's expedition took him first to Florida and then along the Gulf Coast to Pánuco, in northern Mexico. This was the first recorded voyage of the Spanish to that area. Garay's efforts to subdue Cortés failed in 1523, when most of the men in an expedition he led against Cortés chose to join the rebel's forces. The unlucky Garay was captured and died in captivity.

In 1526, still annoyed by Cortés's independence, Velásquez commissioned Pánfilo de Narváez to take control of a large area along the northern coast of the Gulf of Mexico west to the Rio de las Palmas, well into Cortés's domain. Narváez received political authority over a vast territory from which he was expected to threaten Cortés. Narváez left Spain in June 1527 with five ships and 600 men, although about 140 stayed in Santo Domingo when the expedition stopped to resupply. After wintering in Cuba they landed at Tampa Bay in April 1528. Interested in finding gold rather than Cortés, Narváez took the main body of his men ashore and set off toward the north, occasionally encountering Indians, but finding no treasure. They reached the Tallahassee area in June, where food was more plentiful, and then continued moving west. In August, they decided to build some boats and sail across the Gulf of Mexico to the safe port of Pánuco. Setting sail in September, they followed the coast, encountering storms and antagonizing resident Indians. Somewhere off the coast of Louisiana, three of the five ships were lost, including the one carrying Narváez; the other two were beached at Galveston Bay in November, stranding about ninety men there.

In one of the great odysseys of history, about a dozen of these men survived and roamed the southwestern countryside for more than seven years. They traveled as far west as southern New Mexico. The last four survivors crossed the Rio Grande River and made their way to Mexico City, arriving in the summer of 1536. One of the survivors, Álvar Núñez

Cabeza de Vaca, wrote expansively about his experience, and his account opened the eyes of Spanish leaders to the possibilities of wealth that might lie north of Mexico.

Cabeza de Vaca and his fellow travelers told stories gleaned from indigenous people they had met about other people farther north who lived in large dwellings and had turquoise, emeralds, and tropical birds. Spanish authorities were impressed and decided to send Hernando de Soto to learn more. De Soto had received Narváez' title to the Gulf Coast territory in 1537 after a profitable career as a conquistador in Peru, and the Spanish were still interested in staking a permanent claim to the area. De Soto's expedition set out from Spain in April 1538 with more than 600 men. After a winter in Cuba, the expedition landed at Tampa Bay at the end of May 1539 and moved north by land, much as Narváez had done. They had frequent clashes with the Indians as they moved into northern Florida. After a winter in Tallahassee, the explorers continued north into present-day Georgia, then northeast into South Carolina, and finally west toward Chattanooga, Tennessee. They arrived there in June 1540, turned south, moved through Alabama all the way to Matula, just north of Mobile, where they fought a major battle with local Indians. That forced de Soto back toward the north, and the expedition spent its third winter on the road in northeastern Mississippi. In the spring of 1541, the party continued westward, crossing the Mississippi River in June and spending most of the rest of that year and the next winter in present-day Arkansas.

By the spring of 1542, the weary de Soto had apparently abandoned his search for turquoise, emeralds, and tropical birds, and the expedition moved south toward the Gulf. Fighting Indians was still a common occurrence. De Soto died in May of a fever, and the survivors agreed to try to get to Pánuco. They wintered in northeastern Louisiana, near the Mississippi River, built barges, and floated down the river in the spring, and after still more conflict with Indians, they reached the Gulf of Mexico in July and Pánuco in September.

Meanwhile, back in Mexico, the viceroy, Antonio de Mendoza, appointed Francisco Vásquez de Coronado governor of Nuevo Galicia, a recently created province on Mexico's west coast. In 1539, Mendoza and Coronado dispatched a missionary, Marcos de Niza, who had also been in Peru, to the north to see what he could find in the way of cities or treasures.

De Niza, ably assisted by a black slave and translator, Esteban de

Dorantes, returned in August with reports about a place called the Seven Cities of Cíbola, comparing it to the fabled Inca cities in Peru. Encouraged, Mendoza and Coronado sent another expedition, this time headed by Melchior Diaz, a military officer, northward. He too reported positively about Cíbola when he returned, and his report convinced Coronado to take an army himself in search of Cíbola.

Coronado's force numbered 350 Spaniards, of whom more than 200 were mounted. In addition, Coronado had 1,300 Indians, an unknown number of additional servants and slaves, and 1,500 horses and mules. Herds of cattle and sheep were brought along to ensure a supply of fresh meat. More supplies were sent by ship up the coast of the Gulf of California. The expedition arrived at Culiacan on March 28, 1540, and at the town of Hawikuh, supposedly a Cíbolan site, on July 7, taking routes that are still in dispute among historians and archaeologists. Although the supply voyage sailed to the junction of the Gila and Colorado Rivers in the summer of 1540, the expedition never made contact with it. Another supply expedition the next year was aborted by a Mixton Indian rebellion in Jalisco.

Meanwhile, Coronado and his men made contact with a smaller group headed by Hernando de Alvarado that included a Pawnee Indian who the Spanish named "Turk," who told the Spanish about other sources of great wealth. Coronado stationed the main body of his expedition in the Sonora Valley in the fall of 1540 prior to moving to winter quarters in the Rio Grande Valley. But he took thirty men with him and continued the search in what is now southeastern Socorro, finding nothing of value.

By early 1541, the lack of supplies had become a serious problem. The Spanish demanded clothes and food from Indian villages and burned and looted them when the Indians proved uncooperative. In April, Coronado directed the expedition toward another rumored golden city, Quivira, leaving the unhappy Indians behind. His force, now numbering about 1,700, moved to the Pecos River, where it met hostile Indians. After diplomacy failed, Coronado bridged the river, continued eastward, and found large herds of bison. The expedition spent the summer of 1541 in the Arkansas River valley, not too far from where de Soto's expedition was exploring, but again it found nothing of consequence.

Coronado planned to continue his wanderings in 1542, still certain he would find gold and the lost city of Quivira. Early in the year, however, he was seriously injured in a riding accident, and after receiving word that another Spanish expedition had been nearly wiped out in an Indian uprising, he decided to return to Mexico, leaving several small parties behind to continue the search. Not until the 1580s did the Spanish mount a large-scale expedition to this area again.

INTERPRETIVE ESSAY
Thomas Clarkin

On Sunday, February 22, 1540, the viceroy of New Spain, Antonio de Mendoza, watched as an expeditionary force assembled for an official review before it set forth to explore *la Tierra Nueva*, the New Land, the unexplored territory to the north of the Spanish Empire. Commanded by Francisco Vásquez de Coronado, the small army of adventurers included some three hundred European soldiers, perhaps a thousand or more Indian allies, and between four and six friars. Fifteen hundred animals, including packhorses and mules to carry supplies and tow the six brass cannons, and sheep and cattle for food, accompanied the expedition. After celebrating Mass, the force gathered to hear Viceroy Mendoza offer a speech in which he spoke of the expeditions goals: the conquest of new lands that would bring the soldiers and Spain great wealth, and the opportunity to bring new souls to God. The men then swore an oath of loyalty to Coronado. The following day they began the journey known as the *entrada* that would last more than two years, and reveal the peoples and places of the American southwest to European eyes for the first time. More than four hundred years after the *entrada*, Coronado's grand failure remains an exciting tale of adventure and exploration that endures as an essential part of the history of the American southwest.

Mendoza spoke of saving souls, and while converting Indians to Christianity was always important to the Spanish, it was the lure of riches that drew men to scramble for a place in the expedition. The viceroy had promised each soldier a land grant in the territory that they claimed for Spain, and the Indians had been guaranteed their fair share. But Coronado's force did not set forth into *la Tierra Nueva* out of a desire for land. They sought the Seven Cities of Cíbola, a civilization of amazing wealth that they believed lay somewhere to the north.

By the time of Coronado, the legend of the Seven Cities was several centuries old. During the eighth century, so the story went, seven Christian bishops fled from invading Moors, sailing west over the ocean.

When they reached the distant island of Antillia, each bishop constructed a magnificent city of gold. In the minds of many Europeans, the story of the Seven Cities of Antillia was no mere folktale. Mapmakers included Antillia on their maps, and during the fifteenth century at least one sea captain planned a voyage to discover the island's exact location.

Upon arriving in the Western Hemisphere, Europeans assumed they were close to Antillia. They did not find the cities of gold, but hope remained, and their dreams gained new life when Álvar Núñez Cabeza de Vaca and his three companions arrived in Mexico City in July 1536. Members of an ill-fated expedition that landed in Florida in 1528, Cabeza de Vaca and his friends were shipwrecked on the Texas coast later that year. For the next eight years they lived among the Indians, wandering through the region until they encountered a party of Spaniards in March 1536. Their arrival astounded the Spanish, who eagerly listened to Cabeza de Vaca's tales of enormous cities to the north, where the people traded turquoise and emeralds for the feathers of tropical birds. He did not claim to have seen such cities, only to have heard of them from Indians that he encountered. Despite Cabeza de Vaca's cautious reports, New Spain was gripped with excitement at the prospect of discovering and conquering what surely must be the Seven Cities.

What were the Indians referring to when they told Cabeza de Vaca of the distant cities of wealth? They may have been referring to trading cultures and kingdoms that existed in various locations in North America, including those of the people known as the Anasazi or pre-Puebloans in the southwest. In addition, historians have pointed out that American Indians had their own myths and legends, one of which concerned a city called the Seven Caves. It is possible that Indians were sharing their own legends with Cabeza de Vaca, who understood them in terms with which he was familiar.

Whatever their origin, the Indian tales of distant lands that Cabeza de Vaca shared held a great appeal for the people of New Spain, who had good reason beyond their belief in the legend of Antillia to accept those rumors as fact. The New World had already yielded a fabulous trove of treasure. Cortés had plundered the cities of the Aztecs less than two decades earlier, and only five years had passed since Francisco Pizarro had conquered the Inca Empire to the south, again capturing vast riches. Surely kingdoms of great wealth and beauty would be found in the north, ripe for the conquistadors bold enough to venture into unknown lands.

Viceroy Mendoza believed so, and in March 1539, he sent the Franciscan friar Marcos de Niza (Fray Marcos) to investigate. One of Cabeza de Vaca's companions, Estevánico, an African, accompanied Fray Marcos, as did a small group of Indians. Fray Marcos returned that summer with thrilling news. He had seen but not entered a city larger than Mexico City that the inhabitants called Cíbola. The people lived in houses that were several stories high and had turquoise decorations on the doorways. In his official report Marcos noted that there were a total of seven such cities. Although he had not seen gold, Indians claimed it was common to the region. Privately, Fray Marcos told people that he had seen idols covered with precious stones.

Fray Marcos did not enter the city because Estevánico, who had gone ahead, had been murdered there. His contemporaries and later generations of scholars have expressed doubts about Fray Marcos and his report. Hernán Cortés dismissed Fray Marcos as a liar, and some historians have claimed that he never saw the city, fleeing in panic when he received word of Estevánico's death and fabricating the details that he later recounted. Others maintain that Fray Marcos probably saw a pueblo, a city constructed by the Indians. The word Cíbola is in all likelihood a mispronunciation of the Zuni word for the area that Fray Marcos visited.

Whether falsehoods or exaggerations, Fray Marcos's reports included two crucial pieces of misinformation. First, the friar portrayed Cíbola as a region of considerable wealth, a depiction certain to fire the Spanish desire to conquer the territory immediately. Second, Fray Marcos claimed that Cíbola was near the sea. This observation led Coronado to rely upon a small convoy of ships following Mexico's western coast to resupply his expedition as he headed northward.

Fray Marcos had been to Peru and seen the riches of the Incas, and his word was enough to generate rumors of golden cities among the inhabitants of New Spain. When Mendoza learned that the conquistador Hernando de Soto was organizing an expedition to search for the Seven Cities by way of Florida, he knew he had to act quickly in order to be the first to lay claim to the riches. He selected Coronado to mount a major expedition into *la Tierra Nueva*. Born in Spain in 1510, Coronado had accompanied Mendoza to New Spain and had served as a provincial governor, a military commander, and as a member of the council in Mexico City. While Coronado organized the land expedition, Hernando de Alarcón prepared the supply fleet. In the meantime Melchior Diaz led a small party north in an effort to confirm Fray Marcos's reports.

The Coronado expedition departed on February 23, 1540. Less than a month later, Diaz met the expedition with some troubling news. Poor weather had prevented him from reaching Cíbola, but the Indians he interviewed made it clear that the settlements were small and contained no gold. Fray Marcos, who was present, argued that Diaz had not gone far enough north, and assured Coronado that they would see the riches of Cíbola in the coming weeks. Satisfied with Fray Marcos's explanation, Coronado ordered Diaz to join the expedition, which in late March reached the Spanish settlement at Culiacán, where the group rested for nearly a month.

While at Culiacán, Coronado decided to split the expedition into two groups. He would lead a small party of perhaps one hundred men north, while the main body, which moved slowly under the weight of supplies, followed at a slower pace. Coronado's force made good time and entered into the present-day state of Arizona in late May. However, supplies were running low, and doubts regarding Fray Marcos's reporting skills grew as the party encountered no evidence that the friar had told the truth. Several men and horses died in the uninhabited region, which the Spaniards called the *despoblado*, the wasteland or uninhabited region. Weary and facing starvation, the advance force encountered Zuni Indians in early July. Finally, on July 7, Coronado and his men laid eyes on Cíbola, and their disappointment knew no bounds.

Schooled in the legends of Antillia, bolstered by the tales of Fray Marcos, and led on by their own greed, Coronado and his soldiers anticipated a city of gold and silver and turquoise. Instead, they saw a small city of stone, the Zuni pueblo of Hawikuh in modern New Mexico. One member of the expedition later recalled that the first reaction of the men was to curse the friar. Despite the crushing realization that he had been misled, Coronado prepared to claim the pueblo for Spain.

Informed by scouts of the approach of the strangers, the Zunis had prepared for the worst. Women and children were sent away, and the ground in front of the pueblo was patterned with lines made from sacred golden cornmeal as a warning not to pass this way. The Zuni men lined the walls of the town as a small group of Spaniards moved toward the town to read aloud a document known as the *requirimiento*.

Spanish law required the conquistadors to explain their mission to the Native peoples by reading the *requirimiento*, which informed the Indians that they must accept Christianity and recognize the Spanish Crown. If they agreed, all would be well. If they refused, their lands would be taken and they would be killed or taken as slaves. The reading of the *requirimiento* satisfied the Spaniards, but meant nothing to people who could not understand Spanish, or in the event that it was translated still could make little sense of it. In any case, the Zunis were unwilling to submit to the demands of strangers whom they regarded as dangerous. When Coronado's men went forth to read the proclamation, the Zunis shot arrows at them.

Why did the Zunis respond with hostility to Coronado's expedition, which at this point was clearly in poor shape after making the arduous journey to the pueblo? Although the Zunis probably had no firsthand acquaintance with these foreigners (other than the unfortunate Estevánico, whom they had killed the year before), they probably knew about the strangers clad in metal. A slave-trading network had developed in New Spain, and Indians throughout the region feared the armored soldiers who kidnapped their people and never returned them. Coronado's men met with arrows because their reputation had preceded them.

Historians have offered an additional reason for the Zunis' refusal to receive the Spaniards with open arms. The expedition arrived during summer ceremonies related to the harvest. The Zunis may have believed that the interruption of the sacred rituals might result in a poor harvest; thus, Coronado unknowingly posed a threat to the well-being of the entire community when he arrived on that summer day in 1540.

The clash at Hawikuh was yet another instance of the collision of European and Indian cultures that was repeated again and again along the Spanish frontier. Although the specifics of each encounter differed in some respects, the meetings between these two very different cultures often resulted in misunderstandings, disagreements, and finally bloodshed. Indians usually suffered the most as a result of these meetings for a number of reasons. The introduction of European diseases decimated their populations and disrupted the social order, and they did not possess the weapons such as the crossbow, the harquebus, and the cannon, which the Europeans used. However, Coronado did not gain much advantage from these two factors. There is no record of widespread epidemic in the region that would have weakened the Indians prior to his arrival. Cannons would prove ineffective against the walls of the pueblos, which were designed as defensive strongholds.

Organization was the key to Coronado's successes against the Indians, and it carried the day at Hawikuh. He ordered his forces to surround the pueblo to prevent any Indians from escaping and had his archers clear the pueblo's terraces of defenders. Although Coronado was knocked unconscious by a stone, his men rallied and through a determined effort entered the pueblo. The Zunis surrendered and departed, and the famished Spaniards found a treasure more valuable than gold, food stores, which they immediately plundered.

Coronado occupied Hawikuh and negotiated a peace with the Zunis, who for the most part kept their distance by staying at pueblos to the east. Determined to achieve success, Coronado had no intention of abandoning his quest. In the following weeks he sent out several small parties to continue exploring. He ordered Melchior Diaz to head south and contact the main body of the expedition. Diaz did so, and then headed west in hopes of finding Alarcón and the supply fleet. Contrary to Fray Marcos's report, Cíbola (now renamed Granada in honor of the hometown of Viceroy Mendoza) was nowhere near water, and the expedition had lost contact with the fleet months earlier.

Diaz reached the Colorado River, where he met Indians who told him they had sighted boats downriver weeks earlier. Diaz and his men hurried south, where they discovered carvings on a tree indicating that letters were buried in a box there. They learned that Alarcón had sailed up the Gulf of California, and had taken small boats several miles up the Colorado River about two months earlier. However, worms were eating the boats, and Alarcón had no choice but to return to New Spain. The expedition would not receive badly needed winter supplies; and to make matters worse, Diaz, a trusted and reliable officer, was killed in a freak accident on the return journey.

Meanwhile, Coronado sent a second expedition to investigate rumors of another seven cities to the west. In what is today northeastern Arizona, Pedro de Tovar and his soldiers met the Hopi Indians, who like the Zunis were not receptive to the strangers. A short battle ensued, after which the defeated Hopis offered assistance to the invaders. Tovar returned to Hawikuh without gold but with news of a great river farther to the west. Coronado then dispatched García López de Cárdenas to find the river and follow it downstream, probably in hopes that he might encounter Alarcón. With the aid of Hopi guides, Cárdenas reached the Colorado River in late September 1540.

He saw what he later described as a brook about six feet wide. The Hopis insisted that it was a mighty river, and indeed it was. Cardenas was viewing the Colorado from the rim of the Grand Canyon, the first European to do so. The Spaniard was unable to fathom the enormous size of the canyon and believed the river to be closer than it was.

Today the Grand Canyon is recognized as one of the natural marvels on the Earth, and as a part of the U.S. National Park system it draws visitors from all over the world. However, Cárdenas and his men left no record indicating that the natural beauty of the canyon awed them. Instead, they regarded it as a gaping wound in the earth that stopped their advance and prevented them from reaching the river. For three days they traveled along the rim of the canyon searching for a path down, until, ironically, a shortage of water forced them to retreat.

Coronado sent a final exploration party to the east. When two Indians arrived from the east offering their friendship, Coronado authorized Hernando de Alvarado to return with them. Remembered only by the nicknames given them by the Spaniards, Cacique and Bigotes spoke of villages that lined a great river and large herds of wild cattle. With the capable assistance of Bigotes, Alvarado and his men met with no opposition from the Indians they encountered on their journey. They visited the pueblo at Acoma, and then proceeded to the river now called the Rio Grande. They named that region, which is now the site of the city of Albuquerque, the province of Tiguex, after the Tigua Indians who lived there. The party then headed north, but soon returned to Tiguex and again headed east.

Alvarado's men visited the home of Bigotes, the pueblo at Pecos, and while there they met an Indian who altered the future and the fate of Coronado's expedition. The man, who was probably a Pawnee captured by the people at Pecos, was nicknamed Turk by the Spaniards. Turk traveled east with the party, perhaps reaching the border of modern Texas, where the Spaniards first saw the amazing herds of buffalo that ruled the grasslands of the high plains. Along the way, Turk told the strangers of great kingdoms to the east that were filled with gold. Unwilling to learn their lesson, the Spaniards seized on these stories as evidence of the fabled Seven Cities.

Historians believe that Turk was describing Indian communities of the Mississippian culture, which were indeed impressive but did not possess gold. Perhaps Turk mentioned the imaginary gold in order to persuade Alvarado to continue eastward, thus giving Turk the opportunity to return home. However, Alvarado rushed back to inform Coronado, and as he hurried west he brought with him Turk, Cacique, and Bigotes in chains to ensure their cooperation.

Coronado had taken a small party south while the main force of the expedition established winter quarters at Tiguex. The Spaniards forced the Indians from one pueblo for their own use. Faced with a serious shortage of supplies because of the failure to meet with Alarcon's fleet, expedition members seized food and clothing from the Tiguas. Relations between the Spaniards and the Indians rapidly worsened, and Cárdenas, who was in charge during Coronado's absence, ordered his men to destroy one pueblo and burn any survivors at the stake. Throughout the winter and into the early spring a brutal war raged along the northern Rio Grande, resulting in the destruction of many villages and the enslavement of an unknown number of Tiguas. The war ended in April, when Coronado set out to Quivira, the golden kingdom of which Turk had spoken.

With Turk acting as a guide, the expedition, which numbered over 1,700, headed east, soon reaching the grasslands of modern Texas. The monotonous landscape offered no markers to measure the distances traveled each day, and Coronado and his men grew disoriented as they crossed the plains. Their confusion was compounded by the fact that Turk was intentionally leading them astray, hoping to lose them in the vast wilderness so that they would never return to harm his people. As a result, to this day historians are uncertain as to the route, the expedition took through Texas.

Frustrated by the apparent lack of progress toward Quivira, Coronado confronted Turk, who admitted his deception. Coronado ordered the main body of the expedition to return to Tiguex and prepare for another winter. He selected a small group of men to continue the search for Quivira, following the directions of an Indian named Ysopete who insisted that the city lay to the north. After several days of travel, the party arrived in what is now central Kansas. There they discovered Quivira, several small villages belonging to the Wichita Indians, whom Coronado dismissed as barbarians. When he discovered that Turk, who was brought along in chains, was attempting to convince the Wichitas to kill the Spaniards' horses, Coronado had him executed.

Coronado spent three weeks exploring Quivira. Fearing the approach of winter weather, he led his men south back to Tiguex in August. During the harsh and unpleasant months of inactivity, Coronado debated a return to Quivira. Yet another Indian, a Wichita called Xabe, insisted that the Spaniards had not searched long enough because there was indeed gold to be found there. But another foray was not to be. Cardenas left the expedition to fulfill family obligations in New Spain, but he soon returned with bad news. Indians in northern Mexico had destroyed the town of Corazones, and the route back to New Spain was in peril. A final stroke of bad luck, a riding accident in which Coronado was almost killed, ensured the end of the expedition, which headed back to New Spain in April 1542.

The expedition, which had departed with great ceremony just two years earlier, was received with little enthusiasm in New Spain. Mounting the expedition had been an expensive effort, and investors discovered that their profits were nonexistent. Coronado returned with only discouraging news of the north. There were no great cities, no gold to plunder, no fortunes to be made. An official investigation of the expedition determined that Coronado had acted responsibly, and no charges were brought against him. Although he again held government positions, the expedition ruined his career and his health. His contemporaries regarded him as a failure, and many noted a change in his personality and a loss of the leadership qualities he had once possessed. He was also weakened physically, and died in 1554 at the age of forty-four.

Was the expedition a failure? If measured by the dreams that Coronado and his men set forth with in 1540, it was surely no success. They intended to find and conquer the Seven Cities of legend, known variously as Antillia, Cíbola, and finally Quivira. The soldiers suffered two years away from family and friends, facing the hardships of travel in unknown territory, hunger, and the danger posed by Indians. All these sacrifices were made for nothing, and although he was officially held blameless many citizens of New Spain held Coronado to be at fault.

However, it is difficult to find failure in an expedition with goals that were founded in legend and rumor. Coronado could not find the fabulous cities of gold because they did not exist, and Viceroy Mendoza, despite his disappointment, knew this. The myth of the Seven Cities lingered on for a while—a 1578 map shows Cíbola in all its golden glory, and at times French and English explorers pondered the existence of a land of wealth in the Western Hemisphere. However, for the most part the dream died with the return of the dusty and bedraggled men who marched back to New Spain in 1542.

The long-term consequences of the expedition's discoveries were minimal. Although accounts of the expedition were written, they were not readily available in New Spain, and within three decades the information that Coronado had brought back with him was largely forgotten. The people of New Spain focused their energies on activities closer to home, especially exploiting the vast silver mines that were discovered in Mexico. The lands to the north were again places of mystery.

The expedition had little impact on the world of the American Indians in the southwest. Archaeologists have discovered no evidence that they adopted any Spanish technology, either in the form of weapons or other material objects such as pottery. Moreover, efforts to convert Indians do not appear to have had any long-lasting effect, and Christianity did not take root among the peoples who listened to the friars during the *entrada*.

Modern scholars have explored two facets of the Coronado expedition; one a curiosity of minor importance, the other more significant. The question of Coronado's route has long been a great historical puzzle, and professional and amateur historians have invested time and effort into retracing his steps. While these studies have revealed the location of pueblos and of certain Indian communities in Texas and Kansas, they tend to satisfy the curiosity more than they offer insight into the Spanish frontier in the sixteenth century.

Coronado's interactions with the Indians of the southwest provide a useful means of understanding the cultural clashes that marked the European arrival in the Americas. Coronado was a conqueror, both in his intent and his method. He wanted to acquire the legendary gold of the north, and he ventured forth with a military force ready to subdue the Native peoples if necessary. His predecessor, Cabeza de Vaca, had been forced to live with the Indians, and in so doing he learned about their cultures and their ways of interacting with the environment. As a result, he gained a great appreciation for the Indians. When he returned to New Spain, he denounced the trade in Indian slaves as unchristian, and he soon earned a reputation for being too kind to Indians.

Coronado and his men depended upon the Indians in a different manner, relying upon their food stocks when their own supplies dwindled. Because they did not respect the Indians, they never learned from them, and the European and American cultures remained distinct and antagonistic. The expedition left in its wake a hatred for the Spanish, which would sour relations between the two peoples for centuries.

However, Spanish attitudes toward the Indians were ambivalent. On the one hand they were a people to conquer and to enslave. On the other hand, they were human beings who possessed souls and needed to be converted to Christianity. These conflicting viewpoints resulted in actions that seem odd or even contradictory today, such as the reading of the *requirimiento* before attacking Indian communities. Two minor events connected to the Coronado expedition reveal the tensions in the Spanish attitudes toward American Indians.

The first was the fate of García López de Cárdenas, who commanded the expedition during Coronado's absence and started the war with the Tigua during the winter of 1541–42. Cárdenas was found guilty of mistreating the Indians, and he spent seven years in prison for his crimes. The second was the decision of Friar Luis de Ubeda to remain at Pecos to minister to the Indians there. (Another friar, Juan de Padilla, returned to Quivira, but historians suspect he was more interested in searching for gold than in saving souls.) About Ubeda there are no such doubts, because Pecos offered no riches. Given the fact that the Indians at Pecos were angry with the Spaniards, Ubeda's decision reflected great courage and dedication to his cause. His fate remains a mystery, but his act reflects a commitment to his faith and to the mission of bringing Christianity to the Indians. Spaniards such as Friar Ubeda make the history of the Spanish frontier a complex tale of which Coronado's *entrada* is a fascinating component.

SELECTED BIBLIOGRAPHY

Bolton, Herbert E. *Coronado on the Turquoise Trail: Knight of Pueblos and Plains.* Albuquerque: University of New Mexico Press, 1949. Bolton's entertaining account of the expedition is considered a classic of historical writing.

Chavez, Angelico. *Coronado's Friars.* Washington, D.C.: Academy of American Franciscan History, 1968. The *entrada* from the perspective of the friars who accompanied the expedition.

Clissold, Stephen. *The Seven Cities of Cíbola.* London: Eyre and Spottiswoode, 1961. A well-written account of efforts to find the fabled seven cities.

Day, A. Grove. *Coronado's Quest: The Discovery of the Southwestern States.* Berkeley: University of California Press, 1964. A biography of Coronado that focuses on the *entrada*.

Flint, Richard, and Shirley Cushing Flint, eds. *The Coronado Expedition to Tierra Nueva: The 1540–1542 Route Across the Southwest.* Niwot, CO: University Press of Colorado, 1997. This collection of essays continues the debate over the route that Coronado took.

Hallenbeck, Cleve. *The Journey of Friar Marcos de Niza.* Dallas, TX: Southern Methodist University Press, 1987. Contains a translation of Friar Marcos's account of his 1539 journey and an essay that is highly critical of Marcos.

Hodge, Frederick W., and Theodore H. Lewis, eds. *Spanish Explorers in the Southern United States, 1528–1543.* Austin: Texas State Historical Association, 1984. This volume contains a translation of Pedro de Castaneda's chronicle of the *entrada*.

Kessell, John L. *Kiva, Cross, and Crown: The Pecos Indians and New Mexico, 1540–1840.* Albuquerque: University of New Mexico Press, 1979. The opening chapter examines the impact of Coronado upon the Pecos Indians.

Riley, Carroll L. *Rio del Norte: People of the Upper Rio Grande from Earliest Times to the Pueblo Revolt.* Salt Lake City: University of Utah Press, 1995. This history of American Indians includes chapters on the *entrada*.

Sauer, Carl Ortwin. *Sixteenth Century North America: The Land and the People as Seen by the Europeans.* Berkeley: University of California Press, 1971. A standard source that includes chapters on Spanish exploration and Coronado.

Speck, Gordon. *Myths and New World Explorations*. Fairfield, WA: Ye Galleon Press, 1979. Readable discussion of the role of myth that includes black and white photographs.

Terrell, John Upton. *Search for the Seven Cities: The Opening of the American Southwest*. New York: Harcourt Brace Jovanovich, 1970. This account is most appropriate for younger readers.

Udall, Stewart L. *Majestic Journey: Coronado's Inland Empire*. Santa Fe: Museum of New Mexico Press, 1987. Places the expedition into the larger context of Spanish exploration and includes beautiful color photographs of locations that the expedition visited.

Weber, David J. *The Spanish Frontier in North America*. New Haven, CT: Yale University Press, 1992. While the discussion of Coronado is brief, this work provides an excellent overview of the Spanish frontier for interested students.

Beſchreibung deſz Vorgebürgs Flo=   I.
ride, da die Frantzoſen anzufahren pflegen, welches von
ihnen das Frantzöſiche Vorgebürg ge=
nannt wirdt.

Als die Frantzoſen das erſte mahl in die Landſchafft Floridam
geſchiffet, ſind ſie an das Vorgebürg, nicht ſonderlich hoch (dann das Uſer eben,
vnd mit ſehr hohen Bäumen bewachſen war) angeländet, Welches dem Frantzöſi=
ſchen Königreich zu Ehren, das Frantzöſiche Vorgebürg, von dem Schiffoberſten,
genannt worden, Ungeſehrlich dreyſſig gradus weit vom Æquatore vnterſcheyden.
Von dannen, als ſie an dem Mitnächtiſchen Uſer her gefahren, haben ſie ein breytes
vnd luſtiges Waſſer antroffen, bey welches Eingang ſie ire äncker eingeſenckt, vff daß ſie es folgenden
Tages deſto beſſer beſchauwen möchten. In der andern Schiffahrt hat der Herr Laudonniere dieſen
Fluß den Delphinerbach genannt, dieweil er in demſelbigen viel Delphin ſchwimmen geſehen. Als ſie
nun an das Geſtade deß Waſſers angefahren, haben ſie daſelbſt viel Indianer gefunden, die ſich da=
hin verſamlet hatten, daß ſie ſie freundlich vnd holdſelig empfiengen: Wie ſie dem auch mit der
That erfahren haben, dann ſie ihrem Oberſten, neben vielen geſchenckten Häuten, auch verhieſſen,
daß ſie ihm ihren König zeigen wolten, der damals mit ihnen nicht auffgeſtanden, ſondern noch auff
vntergeſträuweten Lorbeern vnnd Dattelbäumen Blättern ſaß, Welcher dem Ober=
ſten eine Haut, von mancherley Thieren, als ob ſie noch lebten, ſehr lu=
ſtig gezieret, ſchenckte.

A iij

This German book illustration from the late sixteenth century gives some idea
of what the French saw when they first arrived in the St. Augustine area in 1564.
(Reproduced from the Collections of the Library of Congress.)

3

The Founding of St. Augustine, 1565

INTRODUCTION

The first Spanish explorer to set foot in Florida was Juan Ponce de León in March 1513. He named what he thought to be an island La Florida, because in the Spanish religious calendar, March was the time of the Feast of Flowers. At the time of Ponce's arrival, about twenty-five thousand Indians, spread among four major tribes, lived in Florida. These were the Calusa, who lived in southwest Florida, the Tekesta, from southeast Florida, the Timucua, from northeast Florida, and the Apalachee, from northwest Florida, the area known today as the Florida panhandle.

The Calusa were seagoing Indians who fished and sailed small boats as far away as Cuba and Hispaniola. They did not cultivate crops, although they did gather roots, dry them, and pound them into flour to make into bread. The Calusa developed a fairly sophisticated social structure, with authority vested in a king who resided in a centrally located village protected by extensive fortifications. The tribe also used slaves, who were members of other tribes taken captive in battle. Within their domain, they developed a system of food storage and distribution, so villages that experienced food shortages could be supplied with dried food from other villages. They were not receptive to Spanish encroachment, killing some of Ponce de León's men in 1513, and Ponce himself in 1521 during his second voyage to Florida.

The Timucua, whose culture can be traced back to 500 B.C.E., built villages along rivers or next to lakes. These villages were fortified and included ceremonial sites, granaries, and public buildings. They ate game and fish, planted small gardens, and collected berries and acorns. Like the Calusa, the Timucua developed a social structure based on matriarchal clans, a system of intertribal alliances, and a class system based on a nobility and commoners.

Of the other two Florida tribes, we know less. The Tekesta Indians lived in southeast Florida. They also harassed the Spanish, although fewer attempts were made to settle in that part of Florida than in other parts. Missionaries claimed some success in converting the Tekesta, but the Indians were still reputed to have killed Spanish sailors shipwrecked in their territory, and those Spaniards who escaped them reported that they were cruel and untrustworthy. Near Pensacola in northwest Florida were the Apalachee, a powerful and united tribe whose antagonism toward Europeans helped prevent the success of colonization efforts in that area.

Previous attempts to colonize Florida before 1565 failed, costing Spain many lives and ships and much money. Spanish explorers spent too much time and energy looking for gold and other symbols of immediate wealth, failed to pacify the Indians, and suffered in the hostile climate and environment. The ill-fated but far-ranging expeditions of both Pánfilo de Narváez and Hernando de Soto in the 1520s and 1530s began as Florida colonization efforts. Narváez, who passed through Florida in 1528, found both the land and the Indians inhospitable. De Soto, whose expedition landed near Tampa Bay in May 1539, also encountered difficulty with Indians and found nothing of value. The dismal fates of these two expeditions led Spain to regard Florida as relatively unimportant in their colonial policies, although the strategic location of the territory and the missionary opportunities among Indians remained factors to be considered.

In 1549, the latter of those two factors was recognized with the mission of Fray Luis Cancer de Barbastro to Florida. He was put ashore near Tampa Bay and killed on the beach in sight of the ship that had taken him there. While Cancer's death encouraged some to want revenge against the Indians, the increasing incidence of shipwrecks off the Atlantic Coast of Florida was also a concern, since nothing could be recovered from these wrecks without settlements on the shore.

The first serious attempt to colonize Pensacola occurred in 1561 when an expedition headed by Tristán de Luna y Arellano arrived. Renaming the place Santa Maria, the de Luna expedition left settlers behind, but two years later, after most of a fleet was destroyed in a storm, the Spanish abandoned Santa Maria, and King Philip II decided to make no further attempts to colonize the inhospitable territory. But when the king learned that an expedition of French Huguenots was on its way to set up a colony in Florida, he changed his mind.

René Goulaine de Laudonnière founded the French colony in Florida. The French foreign minister, Gaspard de Coligny, had sponsored the expedition in the hope that the colony could be used as a base from which French ships could raid Spanish fleets carrying treasure back to Europe. Laudonnière and 300 colonists, many of whom were French Huguenots, arrived at the mouth of the St. John's River (which they named the River of May) in April 1564, established good relations with the Indians, and built a fort on the river bank, naming it Fort Caroline in honor of the French king, Charles IX.

Despite its auspicious beginnings, the French colony soon encountered serious problems. Laudonnière proved to be an autocratic leader who also angered the Indians by meddling in their affairs. By December, some colonists were ready to go home, while others were refitting two ships to harass the Spanish. Before they could leave, however, another French fleet, led by Jean Ribault, arrived to reinforce Fort Caroline. Ribault, moreover, had come to replace the discredited Laudonnière, who had been recalled to France.

Philip II, concerned about the threat to Spanish shipping that the French colony represented, dispatched an expedition under Captain-General Pedro Menéndez de Avilés to Florida to oust the French and establish a Spanish colony in the same area. Menéndez left Santo Domingo, the Spanish settlement on Hispaniola, in August 1565 with five ships and 800 people, mostly soldiers and sailors.

Menéndez and his party arrived at a place thirty-five miles south of the French settlement on September 5, 1565, and founded a colony called St. Augustine, named for the saint on whose day they first sighted the place. There they met members of a Timucua Indian tribe, who hated the French for having allied themselves with a rival tribe. The Timucua gave Menéndez information about the French settlement, and the Spanish captain sailed up the coast to the mouth of the St. John's River. Four French ships, under Ribault's command, hastily set sail from the French settlement, and a conflict was avoided when the faster French ships escaped. Ribault then decided to attack the Spanish at their landfall, St. Augustine. He nearly succeeded in destroying the Spanish ships, but at a crucial moment, a sudden storm developed and forced the French ships away.

Menéndez then took his troops across land with an Indian guide, surprised the French, and captured Fort Caroline, killing everyone except women and children under the age of fifteen in the process. Meanwhile, a hurricane had driven the four French ships onto the beach several miles away, where they were wrecked. The survivors appealed to Menéndez for mercy, but the Spaniard ordered most of them killed. Altogether 358 of the 544 French sailors, including the unlucky Ribault, were summarily executed on a sand dune that became known as Matanzas, or Place of Killing. With these executions, the French presence in Florida was ended, and Spanish control of the St. Augustine area was ensured. Fort Caroline was rebuilt and renamed San Mateo.

Although the Spanish colony at St. Augustine survived, other attempts at colonization in Florida did not, and Menéndez's efforts to ally himself with other Indian tribes were also unsuccessful. Menéndez, who had financed much of the expense of colonizing St. Augustine with his own money, had to be sustained in his last years by a royal subsidy and died in poverty in 1574.

The Jesuits first undertook religious conversion in Florida, but they left in 1572, and Franciscan monks took their place. The Franciscans claimed to have won thirteen thousand souls for Christ, but many clerics lost their lives in the process, and the Indians never were assimilated into Spanish colonial life, as they were in other parts of Spanish America.

As happened everywhere else in the Spanish American empire, disease took a heavy toll on the Indian population. Prior to the settlement of St. Augustine, other efforts to create a permanent settlement in Florida had brought deadly disease to Indians in the Pensacola area. In St. Augustine in 1586, the captain of the *Primrose*, a ship in Sir Francis Drake's English fleet, reported, "The wilde people at first comminge of our men died verie fast and said amongst themselves, it was the Englisshe God that made them die so fast" (quoted in Cook, p. 95). Since many of Drake's men died at the same time, this epidemic was probably typhus, a disease to which Europeans had no special immunity.

St. Augustine experienced other epidemics in 1596, 1613–17, and 1649. Franciscans missionaries reported that the epidemic that broke out in 1613 killed perhaps half the population of some tribes, noting that "these deaths have taken great harvests of souls for heaven" (quoted in Cook,

p. 192). The 1649 epidemic, an outbreak of yellow fever, killed the governor of Florida, two treasury officials, and a number of military officers and missionaries in addition to countless numbers of Indians.

For most of the colonial period, St. Augustine was little more than a large, stout fort and the inhabitants were quite dependent on the home government for most of their supplies. Not until the late seventeenth century did the Spanish colonists discover the economic feasibility of cattle raising inland from the fortress town.

INTERPRETIVE ESSAY
Blake Beattie

For most Americans, "colonial America" remains a distant and unvisited country, known chiefly through a few vivid images emblazoned on the American mythic consciousness. The legend of Pocahontas; the first Thanksgiving; the Salem witch trials: these are the remembered emblems of a national formation that played itself out in Virginia plantations and quaint New England villages lying under the white steeples of austere Congregational churches, guided by men with names like John Alden, William Bradford, Roger Williams, and John Smith. Simply put, while few Americans have more than a passing acquaintance with the history of America's European settlement, most would agree that the process began when the first English settlers arrived in Jamestown in 1607 and the Pilgrims landed at Plymouth Rock in 1620, inaugurating an American colonial experience that is essentially English, centered in New England and Virginia, and vigorously Protestant.

This perception has been challenged over the past generation by historians who stress the importance of groups like America's Native peoples or African slaves in shaping American nationhood. Yet even the revisionists, with their heightened consciousness of the "other" in the national history, often overlook the fact that the critically important process of European exploration and settlement, by which America became possible as an historical and a political entity, began not in the north with the English, but in the south with the Spaniards. The first permanent European settlement in what would become the United States of America was a fort christened San Augustin or St. Augustine, by a Founding Father named Pedro Menéndez de Avilés. Two decades would pass before the English settled Roanoke Island. By the time Virginia Dare was born at that ill-fated colony, becoming the first English child born in the Americas, a generation had grown up in Spanish Florida and would still be there long after Virginia and the other 117 Roanoke settlers vanished from history the following year. If it is true that Spain eventually lost the contest for North America to France and especially England, her cultural legacy has endured without interruption in the American southwest and parts of the southeast for four centuries. More importantly, the contest for North America might never have taken place without Menéndez de Avilés's *empresa en la Florida* and the establishment of a Spanish foothold in the New World north of the Rio Grande.

Ironically, the foundation of St. Augustine came about almost accidentally, as an act of desperation, three years *after* the king of Spain had decided to abandon efforts to settle Florida. The Spaniards had attempted to colonize the territory they called La Florida ever since the expedition of Juan Ponce de León in 1513. Contrary to popular belief, the aging veteran of Columbus's second voyage sought not a legendary fountain of youth, but a discovery that would make him as famous as Columbus. What he found instead was financial ruin and a fatal wound from an Indian arrow in 1521. Ponce de León's experience proved portentous for the next two generations of Florida's would-be *conquistadores*. Pánfilo de Narváez (d. 1528) and Hernando de Soto (d. 1542) squandered fortunes, reputations, and ultimately their own lives in picaresque but fruitless quests for gold-laden cities like the ones that Narváez had seen in Mexico and de Soto had plundered while serving under Pizarro in Peru. In 1549, the Dominican friar Luis Cancer de Barbastro and three confrères were martyred while attempting to missionize the Timucua Indians. A decade later the viceroy of Mexico, Luis de Velasco, sent Tristán de Luna y Arellano to found a settlement near Pensacola Bay. Luna lost a third of his 1,500 men and five of his thirteen ships before he was relieved of his command; his successor, Angel de Villafañe, abandoned the colony after a hurricane ravaged his fleet in June 1561. In the aftermath of the debacle, Spain's King Philip II reluctantly declared in September 1561 that the Crown would no longer sponsor colonial initiatives in La Florida.

Spain's involvement in Florida might well have ended then had not the exigencies of dynastic politics driven Philip's French rivals to take advantage of the situation. Since the time of Philip's father, Charles of

Habsburg (1500–1558), France and Spain had been divided by a bitter enmity. Charles stood heir to a remarkable inheritance: from his maternal grandparents, the famous Spanish monarchs Isabella of Castile and Ferdinand II of Aragon, he inherited the Spanish Crown in 1516; after the death of his paternal grandfather, Emperor Maximilian I, he ruled the Holy Roman Empire as Emperor Charles V. The sum of Charles's inheritances—the largest in European history—entailed a collection of satellite states throughout central and eastern Europe and a colonial empire with holdings on four other continents. The vast scope of Charles's power alarmed his European contemporaries, but none more than the Valois kings of France, who found themselves hemmed in by Habsburg patrimonies to the south and to the east. King Francis I fought—and lost—four wars against Charles over disputed territories in Burgundy and Italy. Discouraged by the spread of Lutheranism in the empire, the devoutly Catholic Charles abdicated his constellation of thrones in 1556, leaving the empire to his brother Ferdinand and Spain to Philip. But the division of Charles's inheritance brought no relief to France. Spain was emerging as Europe's greatest military power at a time when France was dangerously destabilized by conflicts between the Catholic majority and the increasingly powerful and assertive Huguenots (French Protestants who followed the teachings of John Calvin). In 1559 Henry II made peace with Philip II at Cateau-Cambrésis, acknowledging Spanish supremacy in Italy in exchange for Burgundy and a much-needed promise of Spanish nonaggression.

Any hope of a rapprochement was extinguished when poor Henry was killed in a joust during the celebrations for the treaty. Franco-Spanish relations deteriorated rapidly in the successive reigns of Henry's three weak sons, particularly during the political ascendancy of Prince Gaspard de Coligny (1519–72), the ambitious and stridently anti-Spanish admiral of France who came to exercise a great influence over young Charles IX between 1560 and 1574. Coligny was a vigorous promoter of overseas colonization who believed that France had done too little to develop its colonial interests in the Americas since Jacques Cartier explored the St. Lawrence basin of eastern Canada in the 1530s and 1540s. He was also a calculating statesman who hoped to strike a blow at Spain's imperial might before it became insuperable. As a Huguenot, he hoped to avert a civil war by uniting France's Catholics and Protestants against their common enemy, Habsburg Spain. For Coligny, the Spanish moratorium on settlement in La Florida was an opportunity too tempting to pass up.

Coligny easily secured royal approval and despatched a fleet to Florida under Jean Ribaut (1520–65), one of France's ablest seamen. On May 1, 1562, Ribaut founded the settlement of Mayport on an island in the St. John's River; a few days later he sailed to Parris Island, off the coast of South Carolina, and established a tiny settlement named Charlesfort, in honor of France's twelve-year-old sovereign. When he returned to France to obtain supplies, however, Ribaut found the kingdom rent by sectarian strife and Coligny out of favor at court. The Huguenot Ribaut eventually decided to try his luck in Protestant England. But Queen Elizabeth I had no desire to be drawn into France's struggle with Spain and had Ribaut cast into prison.

Without material relief, Ribaut's settlements foundered. Charlesfort was abandoned after a fire destroyed its few remaining supplies, and a mutiny broke out at Mayport. The French settlement was on the brink of abandonment when Coligny, restored to royal favor after the Peace of Amboise in March 1563, sent forth a relief expedition under the Huguenot nobleman René Goulaine de Laudonnière, a veteran of Ribaut's first voyage. Upon his arrival in April 1564, Laudonnière immediately set about the construction of a stout, triangular fort not far from Mayport, on a low bluff overlooking the south bank of the St. John's River.

Philip II had long been aware of the French expeditions into Spanish Florida and made no secret of his outrage at Colingy's audacity. Still, prior to the Laudonnière expedition, Philip had hoped to resolve the matter diplomatically. The construction of Fort Caroline, however, forced him to act more decisively. A fortress on Florida's strategic northeast coast would provide a base from which swift French corsairs could strike at sluggish Spanish treasure fleets in the Gulf of Mexico. Reversing his decision of September 1561, Philip now concluded that the French fort had to be destroyed and Florida secured for Spain, at all costs.

The man he selected to lead the venture was Pedro Menéndez de Avilés (1519–74). One of twenty children born to a noble family from Asturias, Menéndez de Avilés had little to expect from the division of his family's modest estate and entered Spain's maritime service as a very young man. With his meager inheritance he purchased a small patrol vessel and quickly established himself as the scourge of the French and Moorish pirates who bedevilled Spanish ships along Spain's Atlantic coast. In 1554 he escorted the future King Philip II to England for his wedding to Queen Mary I; five years later, he commanded the royal guard, which conducted the king safely from Flanders to Spain after the negotiations at Cateau-Cambrésis. In 1559, a grateful Philip II named him captain general of Spain's East Indian fleet. But Menéndez de Avilés had powerful enemies in the merchants' guilds and in the *Casa de Contratación*, the regulatory council founded by Queen Isabella in 1503 to all trade conducted to and from the Spanish West Indies. At their instigation, Menéndez de Avilés was arrested on a charge of smuggling upon his return to Spain in June 1563. He was languishing in a Seville prison, on the brink of political and financial ruin, when he managed to convince his royal patron to grant him the license to settle La Florida in March 1565.

The *conquistadores* of the previous generation claimed to have acted *por dios, oro y gloria*—for God, gold, and glory. Like them, Menéndez de Avilés was driven by official, personal, and spiritual motives. As *adelantado* (the military-governor of a frontier province), he meant to secure La Florida for Spain; as a father, he desperately hoped to find his only son, Juan, who had disappeared while commanding a royal armada near Bermuda in 1563; as a fervent Catholic and a commander of the ancient crusading order of the Knights of Santiago de Compostela, he intended to expel the French heretics from lands that had belonged to Spain for more than fifty years. And so, on June 29, 1565, Menéndez de Avilés boarded his 900-ton flagship, *San Pelayo*, and led a magnificent fleet of nineteen ships and 1,500 souls out of the harbor at Cádiz.

Initially, Menéndez de Avilés seemed no more likely to succeed than any of his predecessors in La Florida. In July his armada was dispersed by storms in the mid-Atlantic; only five of his ships managed to reach Puerto Rico at the beginning of August. Moreover, the indefatigable Ribaut, released from his English prison, had beaten Menéndez de Avilés in a desperate race across the Atlantic and assumed command of Fort Caroline. When Menéndez de Avilés reached the mouth of the St. John's River at the end of August, he was dismayed to find the French fort defended by five bristling warships. In no position to engage the French ships, Menéndez de Avilés withdrew to a natural harbor some forty miles to the south. He had first seen the site on August 28—the feast day of Saint Augustine—and so he named his camp San Augustín. When the armada's Franciscan chaplain Francisco López Mendoza de Grajales celebrated Mass there on September 8, America's oldest continually inhabited city was born.

But the Spaniards had not heard the last of Ribaut. Determined to destroy the Spanish fleet, he sailed into the mouth of San Augustín harbor and might well have defeated the unprepared Spaniards but for a sudden storm, which drove his ships far to the south and wrecked them along Cape Canaveral. Now utterly convinced of God's favor, Menéndez de Avilés took the offensive with a spectacular exploit. Leaving his brother Bartolomé in charge of the camp, Menéndez de Avilés led 500 soldiers on a gruelling four-day march through torrential rains and waist-deep swamps to Fort Caroline. At dawn on the fifth day, the Spaniards attacked, completely overwhelming the unsuspecting French garrison. The women and children were spared, but some 130 French soldiers were put to the sword. Only a handful of men, including Ribaut's son and the rather unheroic Laudonnière, managed to escape by sea. Menéndez de Avilés rechristened the fort San Mateo to honor the apostle on whose feast day (September 21) it had been captured.

The final stages of the conflict were swift, bloody, and predictably one-sided. The survivors of Ribaut's wrecked fleet, unaware that Fort Caroline had fallen and hoping to rejoin their comrades, managed to come within twenty miles of San Augustín before the Spaniards fell upon them in early October. A few managed to escape into the wilderness, only to be captured a month later; the rest of the exhausted French party surrendered in two groups to the smaller Spanish force with only minimal resistance. Menéndez de Avilés and his vice admiral, Diego Flores de Valdéz, had the French prisoners marched across the sand dunes in groups of ten and executed. Of between 150 and 300 men, only twelve Catholics and twelve military musicians were spared. The valiant Ribaut was despatched with a knife to the belly and a pike-thrust through the heart. The site still recalls the ferocity of the Spanish victory in the name Matanzas (Spanish for "massacres") Inlet. La Florida was Spanish once again.

In the conquest of Florida, Menéndez de Avilés brought to bear all of the ruthlessness and daring what had established him as the greatest Spanish naval commander of his day. He soon discovered, however, that the development of a colony there would require more than the skills of a *conquistador*. Each of the Florida settlements founded by Menéndez de Avilés' predecessors had fallen into dereliction within a very short time of its establishment. The failure of the Florida settlements baffled and frustrated their sponsors in Mexico City and Madrid. How could Spain subdue the great empires of the Aztecs and Incas so quickly, yet fail repeatedly in its attempts to colonize a land as comparatively backward and underdeveloped as La Florida?

In fact, the answer lay in the very backwardness, which the Spaniards attributed to Florida. Cortés and Pizarro had overwhelmed advanced, urbanized pre-Columbian states, at least in part with superior military

technologies. The subsequent administration of those states was relatively easy, for both Mexico and Peru had sophisticated, centralized governmental systems not unlike the one that existed in sixteenth-century
Spain. In Mexico, peoples scattered over thousands of square miles had
rendered tribute and obedience for centuries to the emperor in Tenoch-
titlán; the Inca cities created social and political unity all along the An-
dean spine of Peru. Once the Aztec and Inca rulers had been defeated,
the Spaniards could assume their place and impose their own colonial
administration on the vanquished states.

The peoples of Florida had no such tradition of extended political
unity. The Tallahassee hills of the north were home to the agrarian Apalachee. The more warlike Timucua inhabited much of the central peninsula. The Ais, Jeaga, and Tekesta lived along the southeastern coast,
while the fierce, sea-going Calusa dominated the southwest. Each nation
was further divided into scores of independent villages. Some *caciques*
(tribal leaders), especially among the Timucua and Calusa, managed to
unite groups of villages into regional confederations, but rivalries within
confederations were often as bitter as those between them. The divisive-
ness and localism of Florida's peoples made it easy for Narváez and de
Soto to cut a bloody swath through the peninsula, but quite impossible
to subdue whole tribes in a single, decisive stroke. And unlike Mexico
or Peru, the native societies of Florida offered no preexisting administrative infrastructures that could be adapted to Spain's colonial strategy.

Menéndez de Avilés proved more than equal to the challenges before
him. Certainly, he was the first of the Florida *conquistadores* to demon-
strate an active interest in the survival of his settlement. He expended
nearly all of his considerable fortune on the Florida enterprise; by one
contemporary account, Menéndez de Avilés spent almost a million duc-
ats on his expeditionary fleet alone. He was also tireless in soliciting
material support from the *grandes* of the Spanish court. Though he held
the governorship of Florida for life, Menéndez de Avilés spent most of
his time after 1568 in Spain courting wealthy investors; indeed, at the
time of his death, he was in Spain on a fund-raising campaign. Unlike
his predecessors, who quickly sacrificed their perfunctory settlements to
the quest for gold, Menéndez de Avilés remained committed to his Florida colony throughout his life.

To maintain his colony, Menéndez de Avilés developed an extended
organizational scheme centered on the heavily fortified towns of San
Augustín and San Mateo, each with a garrison of 250 men. On the South
Carolina coast the Spaniards constructed a third fort, Santa Elena, with

a garrison of 150, to guard against French attempts to rebuild Charles-fort. Initially, San Augustín appeared the least viable of the three, with its marshy terrain and open, vulnerable harbor. But in 1568, the French privateer Dominique de Gourgues attacked and destroyed San Mateo; the fort was rebuilt and reoccupied, but only briefly. Twenty years later, Santa Elena was abandoned and destroyed by its own garrison after Spain accepted the inevitability of an English settlement in the Carolinas. By 1600, San Augustín was the only major fortified settlement in the territories of Spanish Florida and the uncontested center of the Spanish colonial network there.

The demographics of sixteenth-century San Augustín betray the town's essentially military character and function. The population in-cluded a significant number of artisans and specialized craftsmen, and virtually every family maintained a small farm with livestock; indeed, in a report of 1602, Governor Gonzalo Méndez de Canço complained about the herds of cattle that ran free through San Augustín's muddy streets. As elsewhere in the Spanish New World, San Augustín's popu-lation was ethnically diverse. It included two distinct groups of Span-iards: immigrants from Spain, who typically held the principal military and civil posts in the community, and *criollos*, Spaniards whose birth in "the provinces" entailed a somewhat humbler social station. Spanish ex-peditions to Florida had always included a few fearless women, but they were invariably far outnumbered by Spanish men. From the outset, in-termarriage and ethnic intermixing (*mestizaje*) were essential to San Au-gustín's survival, though less so than in other parts of New Spain, and Hispano-Indian *mestizos* quickly came to comprise a substantial group within the community. At San Augustín the population also included native Floridians and Africans, many but by no means all of whom were slaves. But for all its professional and ethnic diversity, San Augustín remained first and foremost a soldier's town. As of 1598, more than a third of the 625 inhabitants were professional soldiers, and virtually the entire male population, with the exception of the clergy, was expected to bear arms in times of crisis. Compared to the English colonies that later grew up in North America, the settlements of Spanish Florida were distinguished by an ethnic diversity still discernible in many parts of the American southeast, yet rarely managed to move much beyond their principally military foundations.

Though San Augustín was hardly a major colonial center on par with Mexico City, Lima, or Havana, it nevertheless commanded the chain of smaller, dependent outposts that Menéndez de Avilés founded to secure

Spain's foothold in what would become the southeastern United States. In the immediate vicinity, San Augustín was defended by a blockhouse at Matanzas Inlet, a watchtower on Anastasia Island, and three small forts (Picolata, San Francisco de Pupo, and Diego) along the St. John's River. Farther afield, the Spaniards maintained a network of less permanent outposts whose location shifted over time according to military exigency. The first were a series of watchtowers, erected by Menéndez de Avilés and his immediate successors along Cape Canaveral and Biscayne Bay to provide an early warning against the incursions of French pirates. A century later, the Spaniards raised a new line of forts on the Gulf Coast and Pensacola Bay when the French began moving into the Mississippi Delta in the 1680s and 1690s. Regardless of their location, however, the coastal forts remained under the authority of the governor at San Augustín, as part of an extended colonial system intended for the maintenance and consolidation of Spanish power on the northern rim of the Caribbean basin.

Following the example of Ribaut, Menéndez de Avilés hoped to guarantee the security of his settlements further by cultivating peaceful relations with Florida's Native population. He enlisted Timucua scouts in the struggle against Fort Caroline and spent much of the next year traveling throughout the peninsula making contact with Native leaders. But Menéndez de Avilés was haunted by the brutal legacy of earlier *conquistadores*, from whom the Florida Indians had learned to fear Spaniards. In the vicinity of San Augustín he had to contend with the hostility of the formidable Timucua Chief Saturiba, an ally of the French who joined forces with Dominique de Gourgues to destroy San Mateo in 1568. Though Menéndez de Avilés managed to establish cordial relations with the Ais, he failed completely to come to terms with the Calusa. He invested considerable time and energy in negotiating a trade compact with the colorful young Calusa *cacique* whom the Spaniards called Carlos. In 1566, Menéndez de Avilés went so far as to feign a marriage to Carlos's sister, "Doña Antonia"—in spite of the fact that he already had a wife in Spain! But Menéndez de Avilés' efforts came to nothing. In the spring of 1567, the Spaniards learned that Carlos was planning a secret attack and killed the unreliable *cacique*. The rival they raised up to take his place, "Don Félipe," quickly proved as hostile as Carlos had been: he was executed at the orders of the *adelantado*'s nephew, Pedro Menéndez de Marqués, for plotting to destroy the missionary settlement of San Antonio in 1570.

Catholic missions, through which the Spaniards hoped to produce both converts and allies, played an important role in New World colonial strategies. Jesuit friars who accompanied the devout Menéndez de Avilés on his voyage established the first successful Spanish missions in La Florida. At the *adelantado*'s urging and often with his personal participation, major Jesuit missions were founded at Guale (in southeastern Georgia) and Orista; in 1570 friar Juan Baptista de Segura led a missionary party as far north as Chesapeake Bay. Menéndez de Avilés provided each missionary with a daily stipend of three *reales* for subsistence, taken from the *adelantado*'s own pocket. Within just a few years of their arrival, the Jesuits had established ten mission centers in La Florida, before a series of setbacks, including the massacre of Segura and his companions in February 1571, convinced them to withdraw from their mission contract in 1572.

The Franciscans who took up their burden the following year proved considerably more tenacious. Though nominally subject to the bishop of Havana, the Florida missions were effectively autonomous; in the century following Menéndez de Avilés' death, the only bishops to visit the province were Juan de los Cabejos Altimirano in 1606 and Gabriel Días Vara Calderón, who undertook a census of the missions in 1674. Freedom from outside interference enabled the Franciscans in Florida to devise missionary techniques that responded to the peculiar circumstances of the region. Preaching a simplified version of the gospel, the friars often adopted native customs as part of their missionary strategy. In 1595, the Franciscans undertook a more systematic missionary program based on the *encomiendas* (mission-farms built on royal land-grants), where resident Indians received instruction in Catholic doctrine, often from *mestizo* friars and sustained the community through collective agricultural labor. By 1655, seventy friars were claiming to minister to more than twenty-five thousand Native Christians in La Florida, chiefly among the Apalachee and the Timucua. In fact, the Spanish mission system was never as successful as the Spaniards had hoped. Most Indian converts were at best tenuously Catholic, and missionaries never managed to secure a permanent foothold south of San Augustín. Even apparently secure mission centers were prone to Indian uprisings like the one that destroyed the important Guale mission in 1597. By 1705 the Spanish mission system had collapsed altogether under pressure from British colonial militias in the Carolinas, leaving only traces of a Spanish Catholic influence on Florida's Native peoples.

The mixed fortunes of the Spanish missions in Florida may be seen as symbolic for the Florida colony as a whole. To a considerable extent, history and geography conspired to keep the Florida colony from evolving beyond a collection of semipermanent frontier forts. In 1570 Florida was placed under the supreme authority of the viceroys of Mexico, who never saw the territory as anything but a first line of defense against French and English aggression in the Caribbean Sea and Gulf of Mexico. The sweeping powers Menéndez de Avilés enjoyed as *adelantado* were not passed on his to successors; as terminally appointed subordinates to the governor-general of Cuba, later governors of Florida were simply unable to operate with the freedom and initiative of their colony's founder. Moreover, fires, famines, storms, and a general mortality rate that prevented population increase for a century consistently plagued the Florida settlements. In 1600, King Philip III ordered the governor of Cuba to conduct hearings into the feasibility of maintaining the struggling Florida settlements at all; only the perennial threat of French or English attack kept colonial authorities from abandoning Florida altogether.

Most critical was the failure of the Florida colony to develop an effectively independent economy. Without gold, silver, and other mineral resources, La Florida failed to excite much interest from wealthy investors in Madrid and Mexico City; the Spaniards seem not to have appreciated the agricultural potential of Florida's lush, subtropical climate. By 1600, the overwhelming majority of Florida's sparse colonial population lived within the walls of San Augustín, leaving the land beyond largely uncultivated and Florida's natural resources untapped. The *encomiendas* supplied the colony with fruit, grain, and cotton; otherwise, La Florida was entirely dependent on the royal *situado* (subsidy), disbursed annually after 1570 to provide for the colony's defenses and for the missions. The *situado* was wholly inadequate for more significant colonial development; at times, its payment failed altogether and the Florida colonists were forced to borrow from officials in Havana, creating a debt whose full repayment remained forever beyond the colony's capacity.

More than a generation after its founding, San Augustín was still a small and primitive frontier settlement of 120 thatched houses; even the Franciscan church, the town's largest and most important building, was built in part of palmetto leaves and straw. Major building projects in the town were invariably military in character and came in response to foreign attacks from the sea, which reinforced the prevailing view in Mexico City and Havana that Florida was a strategically essential but economically marginal frontier on the peripheries of Spain's New World empire. After Sir Francis Drake attacked and burned the town in 1586, Governor

Hernando de Miranda began the costly fortification of the harbor; the massive stone fortress of San Marcos, which still stands watch over the harbor today, was built at the command of Governor Francisco de la Guerra y de la Vega after the destructive raid of the English pirate Robert Searles in 1668. So long as they remained essentially military posts, neither San Augustín nor its dependent settlements could develop the diversified and professionally specialized population base necessary to colonial self-sufficiency.

But even if Spanish Florida never quite lived up to its founder's expectations, it would nevertheless be a mistake to underestimate the colony's significance. Animated by the tenacious spirit of its founder, San Augustín endured often astonishing hardships to become—as any inhabitant of St. Augustine will proudly attest—the oldest continually inhabited city north of the Rio Grande. While more ambitious colonial ventures elsewhere in North America collapsed in the face of lesser adversities, La Florida weathered remarkable hardships to retain its institutional integrity for two centuries. Pedro Menéndez de Avilés was followed by a succession of forty royally appointed governors who ruled Spanish Florida from 1565 until the British took control of the territory under the Peace of Paris in 1763. After the American Revolutionary War, Florida was returned to nominal Spanish control by the Treaty of Paris (1783), until the territory was annexed in the Adams-Onís Treaty of 1819. Until then, San Augustín and its satellites offered incontrovertible evidence that the North American wilderness could sustain a European colony, so long as its colonists were willing to endure the attendant challenges. Soon after San Augustín's foundation, the wealth of the colonial empire La Florida helped to defend would all but compel Spain's European neighbors to seek their own colonial fortunes in North America. While none of Spain's colonial rivals in the Americas would adopt the Florida model outright, all of them would borrow elements of Spanish colonial government (particularly in terms of military administration), and all would profit from the lessons of the Spanish experiment. Most importantly, as the French, the Dutch, and above all the British came to challenge Spain's domination in the New World, they would create global empires that would not only redefine the bases of power in Europe, but, in the process, lay the foundations of American nationhood.

SELECTED BIBLIOGRAPHY

Axtell, James. *The Indians' New South: Cultural Change in the Colonial Southeast.* Baton Rouge: Louisiana State University Press, 1997. A study of the impact of the Europeans on the southeastern Indians between 1500 and 1700.

Barrientos, Bartolomé. *Pedro Menendez de Aviles, Founder of Florida.* Trans. Anthony Kerrigan. Gainesville: University of Florida Press, 1965. Composed by a prominent Spanish scholar in 1568, this lively and highly informative biography traces Menéndez's life and career up to December 1567.

Cook, Noble David. *Born to Die: Disease and New World Conquest, 1492–1650.* Cambridge, England: Cambridge University Press, 1998. A careful analysis of the depopulating impact of European disease on Native Americans.

Deagan, Kathleen, et al. *Spanish St. Augustine: the Archaeology of a Colonial Creole Community.* New York: Academic Press, 1983. Seven archaeologists examine different aspects of settlement and society in St. Augustine from the sixteenth through eighteenth centuries.

Laudonnière, René. *Three Voyages.* Trans. Charles E. Bennet. Gainesville: University Presses of Florida, 1975. Laudonnière's thorough and fascinating account of the French experience in Florida provides a valuable corrective to Barrientos's panegyric of Menéndez.

Lorant, Stefan. *The New World; the first pictures of America, made by John White and Jacques Le Moyne and engraved by Theodore De Bry, with contemporary narratives of the Huguenot settlement in Florida, 1562–1565, and the Virginia colony, 1585–1590.* New York: Duell, Sloan and Pierce, 1946. This interesting collection of materials includes two eyewitness accounts of the French colony in Florida by the artist Jacques LeMoyne and the carpenter Nicolas LeChalleux, illustrated with forty-three marvelous engravings of Florida's Indians and fauna by Theodore De Bry, based on LeMoyne's own paintings.

Lowery, Woodbury. *The Spanish Settlements within the Present Limits of the United States. Florida, 1562–1574.* New York: Russell and Russell, 1959. First published in 1911, Lowery's comprehensive account, based on extensive consultation of the materials in Ruidíaz's *La Florida*, remains the definitive narrative of the establishment of the Spanish colony in Florida.

Lyon, Eugene. *The Enterprise of Florida: Pedro Menendez de Aviles and the Spanish Conquest of 1565–1568.* Gainesville: University Press of Florida, 1976. This extremely well-researched monograph examines both the founding of the Spanish colony in Florida and the political processes that underlay it.

McEwan, Bonnie G., ed. *The Spanish Missions of La Florida.* Gainesville: University Press of Florida, 1993. This collection of sixteen essays by archaeologists examines a wide range of topics concerning life in the Spanish missions.

Milanich, Jerald T. *Florida Indians and the Invasion from Europe.* Gainesville: University Press of Florida, 1995. Examines the European settlement of Florida from the Indian perspective on the basis of extensive archaeological research.

Reitz, Elizabeth Jean, and C. Margaret Scarry. *Reconstructing Historic Subsistence, with an Example from Sixteenth-Century Spanish Florida.* Glassboro, NJ: Society for Historical Archaeology, 1985. This relatively short monograph offers a fascinating and thorough, though highly technical, investigation of the relationship between environment and diet in early Spanish Florida.
Sauer, Carl O. *Sixteenth-Century North America. The Land and the People as Seen by the Europeans.* Berkeley: University of California Press, 1971. A general survey that draws heavily from contemporary accounts; Part III is most useful for those interested in the Spanish foundation of St. Augustine.
Tebeau, Charlton W. *A History of Florida.* Coral Gables, FL: University of Miami Press, 1971. Chapters 2, 3, and 4 provide a concise discussion of the Spanish experience in Florida, placed in the larger context of the state's history.
Weber, David J. *The Spanish Frontier in North America.* New Haven, CT: Yale University Press, 1992. This lively, well-researched and eminently accessible work tells the story of the Spanish presence and significance in North America.

Early English Colonization Efforts, c. 1584–1630

INTRODUCTION

The first sanctioned English venture to America came with the voyages of an Italian, Giovanni Caboto, better known as John Cabot, at the end of the fifteenth century. Cabot was probably the first European to sail along the coast of eastern North America and recognize it for what it was, a previously unknown continent. As a young man living in Italy, Cabot plied the Mediterranean as a merchant seaman. He went to England around 1484 (some scholars believe it was as late as 1495) and settled in Bristol, already an important seafaring community, where he learned about Iceland and Greenland and the possibility of a passage to the rich lands of the Orient.

In 1496, King Henry VII of England sanctioned Cabot's first voyage of exploration. That year, he made a relatively short voyage that probably did not take him farther than Iceland. In 1497 and 1498, he made two longer voyages in search of a route to Asia.

During his first voyage, from May to August 1497, Cabot reached Labrador and possibly Newfoundland. On his 1498 voyage, sponsored by King Henry and a group of English merchants, he sailed farther to the south and reached the east coast of what is now the United States. Cabot died on this voyage, but his son Sebastian returned to England and spent

A world's fair known as the Jamestown Tercentenary Exposition celebrated the tercentenary of
the founding of Jamestown in 1607. (Reproduced
from the Collections of the Library of Congress.)

the rest of his life aggrandizing his own accomplishments at the expense
of his father's and thoroughly confusing the historical record. Nevertheless, Cabot's voyages did open the door to the possibility for English
exploitation of the New World. England, however, was not yet ready to
take that step.

By the middle of the sixteenth century, England was on the verge of
having the capability to colonize overseas. An economic revival in Europe increased demand for cloth, which at that time, meant wool. England was ideally suited for raising sheep, and the process of creating
enclosed pastureland began. This displaced serfs who had been utilized
as farm laborers and contributed to a late sixteenth-century phenomenon
of excess labor and insufficient food. Wool exports, meanwhile, were
creating a surplus of capital in England that could be used for investing
in, say, a colonization venture.

This economic situation helped create the conditions that produced
colonizing efforts in competition with other states in Europe. By the late
sixteenth century, English merchants were also involved heavily in the
export of finished cloth, a more expansive market than wool. They were
also developing coastal and overseas shipping operations and ultimately,

de facto control of England's foreign trade. This made the merchant class a powerful force in English society and the element necessary for successful colonization.

Not only did the merchants provide the means for colonization, but they also determined the nature and purpose of the colonies that would be established. When it became apparent that England's colonies were not going to yield the treasures in gold and silver that the Spanish colonies did, commerce was the only practical rationale for establishing colonies. From the beginning, English merchants assumed that their colonies would provide raw materials for England's manufacturing economy and markets for England's finished products.

Colonization efforts on the part of the English might have come earlier had it not been for the religious situation in Europe in the mid-sixteenth century. Europe was in the midst of the Protestant reformation, which was producing much political instability because of the intense rivalry between Protestants and Catholics. As a newly Protestant state, thanks to Henry VIII's insistence on several marriages to try to produce a male heir, England was divided between those like Elizabeth I (queen 1558–1603), loyal to her father's religion, and Catholics who continued to place their faith in Rome. Given the domestic situation, as well as the threat posed by Catholic Spain and Catholics in France (itself rent by religious strife), Elizabeth had no time or interest in colonial ventures early in her reign. Toward the latter years of the century, however, the situation within England stabilized, while the rivalry with Spain intensified and grew hostile, factors that produced more interest in extending the competition with Spain into the colonial area.

At the same time, however, Spain was England's best foreign trade customer, and until English merchants found other markets, Spain had to be mollified. These new markets could be developed with American colonies, and as interest in that alternative grew, so did the deterioration of Anglo-Spanish relations, culminating in the defeat of the Spanish Armada in 1588.

By 1588, English sea captains were finding their way to North America in increasing numbers. In the 1570s, Francis Drake and Martin Frobisher skirted the Western Hemisphere in the elusive search for more treasures beyond. The first serious effort to establish a colony in North America was that of Sir Walter Raleigh, who launched an expedition in April 1584. Sailing north of their intended course, the colonists passed the North Carolina coast and made landfall north of Cape Hatteras near

Roanoke Island. The local Indians were hospitable, the food was good and plentiful, and the prospects for a successful colony appeared excellent.

The following year, seven ships under the command of Richard Grenville landed at nearby Pimlico Sound. This time, the loss of a silver cup led to the burning of an Indian village and continued trouble with the natives. A party was left over the winter of 1585–86, however, and survived quite well. In 1586, the Indians' hospitality began to wear thin, and when Drake arrived in June with a veritable fleet of twenty-three ships, the Pimlico settlers chose to return to England.

In July 1587, a new band of colonists came to Roanoke Island. Poorly supplied and inexperienced, they were left to their own devices. By the time a relief expedition returned to Roanoke Island in August 1590, there was no trace of the colony or any of its inhabitants. This put a damper on new colonization efforts for a number of years, although much interest had been generated by the efforts that were made.

Between the 1580s and the formation of the Virginia Company in 1606, the geographer Richard Hakluyt kept interest in colonization alive through his writings about the subject and its importance to England's future national greatness. Only colonies could free England from economic dependence on Spain and provide security by means of allowing the construction of strategic outposts to protect shipping. The idea of converting natives to Christianity and thus pleasing God also worked its way into the equation.

The goal was finally satisfied with the chartering in 1606 of the Virginia Company. The company's purpose was to establish colonies along the Atlantic Coast of America between 34 and 45 degrees north latitude. In 1607, the first representatives of this company landed near the mouth of the James River in present-day Virginia and named their settlement Jamestown, after King James I. On their agenda were the multiple objectives of searching for valuable minerals, looking for a northwest passage to the riches of the Orient, persuading the Indians to be good neighbors, customers, and Christians, and laying the groundwork through agriculture and town-building for a permanent community. When neither gold, nor silver, nor a northwest passage was found in the first year or so, the company changed course and concluded that the only way Jamestown could survive was through a much greater infusion of both capital and settlers. In 1609, the Virginia Company became a public joint-stock company to raise both money and potential settlers. By advertising financial incentives and hinting that investors would participate in the decisions of the company, the Virginia Company eventually attracted the people and money it needed to survive, especially after the move toward extensive tobacco production in 1617. The rapidly growing market for tobacco in England created interest in acquiring land in Virginia, and between 1617 and 1622, the colony grew from 400 to 4,500.

If commerce were the principal motivation for the Virginia settlers, religion served to inspire the earliest New England settlements, although that was not the original intention. In 1602, the *Concord*, captained by Bartholomew Gosnold, anchored off the coast of present-day Maine. This expedition, the first since the disappearance of the Roanoke Island colonists, intended to establish a colony through which the economic resources of the surrounding area could be exploited. The small band of colonists encountered friendly Indians almost immediately, but the task that lay before them was simply overwhelming, and they sailed home after five weeks ashore.

Gosnold made a positive report about the land he had seen, however, and in 1607, another expedition made its way to the shores of Maine, making landfall near the Kennebec River. The colonists built a small fortified village and entered into trade with local Indians, but they were unable to cope with the severe winter weather and returned to England the following spring.

Thus it was the fate of the Pilgrims to create the first permanent settlement in New England in 1620. The Pilgrims were religious refugees who were known as Separatists in England. They believed that the split from the Roman Catholic Church that King Henry VIII had engineered had not gone far enough in liturgical reform. They wanted to "purify" the church by eliminating all ceremonies reminiscent of Catholicism. Some Puritans preferred to fight for reform from within the church, while others felt it necessary to separate themselves from the established church and form their own church. This was not acceptable to the English government. One group of Separatists, after a good deal of legal harassment, found its way to the Netherlands, where freedom of worship was accepted. They stayed in the Netherlands for eleven years, but always felt like exiles, and consequently determined to go to America.

The Pilgrims, as they called themselves, appealed to the Virginia Company of London for a patent, which would give them the right to settle within the territory the company controlled. They also made some financial arrangements with Thomas Weston, a London ironmonger who was seeking investment opportunities. Weston helped the Pilgrims obtain their patent from the Virginia Company and offered to subsidize their expedition, but in return he demanded joint ownership of everything built or produced in the colony for a period of seven years. The details of the arrangement were still unsettled when the Pilgrims left the Netherlands for England, where their ship, the *Mayflower*, was being prepared. Last minute negotiations with Weston broke down, and he withdrew further financial support. The determined Pilgrims proceeded on their own.

The *Mayflower* arrived in Provincetown harbor, at the tip of Cape Cod, on November 11, 1620, but the company moved to Plymouth Bay in early December. During the winter that followed, nearly half the 102 men and women died, and the settlement barely eked out an existence. With the help of friendly Indians, the Plymouth colony did better the next year and were heartened when a group of thirty-six new settlers arrived in November. But the newcomers, who had brought no supplies with them, depleted the available food, and the colony passed another difficult winter. After 1622, however, their fortunes improved, and its survival was ensured.

In 1630, another Puritan colony was established under the auspices of the Massachusetts Bay Company. Here the motive for colonization was again less commercial and more religious. Led by John Winthrop, whose vision for the colony is explored in the interpretive essay for this chapter, the Massachusetts Bay colony grew rapidly in the 1630s, finding its success in good planning, substantial capital, and political influence back in England. Even so, the colonists needed aid from Indians occasionally when crop yields were low. Still, the colony attracted thousands of new settlers during its first decade, and new villages sprung up along the Massachusetts coast and the rivers that emptied into the bays. Settlers spread into present-day Connecticut and in 1643, the four Puritan colonies of Massachusetts Bay, Plymouth, Connecticut, and New Haven loosely organized themselves into the New England Confederation in order to cooperate in regional defense matters against the French to the north, the Dutch to the west, and the Indians all around them.

INTERPRETIVE ESSAY
Rick Kennedy

In the spring of 1630, John Winthrop composed and delivered one of the most famous speeches in American history, "A Model of Christian Charity." Winthrop was the head of the Massachusetts Bay Company, a corporation that organized a crossing of the Atlantic to establish an English colony. His goal, at its core, was simple. He wanted to create a society out of towns that were economically, politically, and religiously prosperous; thereby, being a model to the world. Adopting an image used by Jesus, his colony was to be a "City upon a Hill" where "the eyes of all people are upon us." Although initially delivered as a speech, "A Model of Christian Charity" was subsequently printed as an essay and widely distributed.

The idea of a watching world may seem a bit egomaniacal; however, a bigger world than Winthrop ever imagined has continued to watch for 370 years. Popular histories of Winthrop's company began to be written within a half century. Within another century, English Whigs and American revolutionaries were regularly referring to the motives and actions of the Puritan migration as they questioned the relationship between England and her colonies. In the nineteenth century, the world really was watching America, and Winthrop's speech came to be thought of as prophecy. In the early twentieth century, Puritan studies became a major cottage industry at American universities, and interest in Puritan society and culture has continued throughout the century. Ronald Reagan, in his first inaugural address as president, quoted Winthrop's famous sentence: "For we must consider that we shall be as a City upon a Hill, the eyes of all people are upon us."

The Puritans of Massachusetts Bay, next to our national Founding Fathers, are probably the most highly studied and talked about group of people in American history. If we consider this, Winthrop and his Puritans are more a city on a hill now than they were then. In this light, it behooves us to look at the "Model of Christian Charity" and see what is in it and in the Massachusetts Bay Company's implementation of it that has such lasting power.

John Winthrop was born in 1588, the year the Spanish Armada fell to the English navy. England was proud and confident during the first decades of his life. Queen Elizabeth's greatness was clear. She had made a weak and fractious country strong and stable. Without recourse to ruinous taxation, military oppression, or draconian politics, Elizabeth had guided the country to greatness by compromise and moderation.

When John Winthrop went to Cambridge University he joined with other pious young men who enjoyed the benefits of Elizabeth's England but were uncomfortable with Elizabethan complacency and compromise. For the young men of Cambridge, Elizabethan wealth and stability left them yearning for something still better. Winthrop and many of his friends became part of an informal network of dynamic people called Puritans who wanted to reform England. The members of this informal network would eventually be leaders in a migration to America and a revolution in England.

After college John Winthrop owned a village named Groton out in what might be called the Kansas of England. Winthrop was a typical village owner. He rented lands to farmers on long-term leases, owned and operated the church, hired the minister, settled local disputes, and encouraged education, family life, and care for any in the community who became destitute. Winthrop was a member of the conscientious ruling elite of England. Men such as he were the backbone of what made rural England good and virtuous. They considered themselves and the people they looked after to be free.

After Elizabeth died in 1603, the Stuart family came to the throne. To people like Winthrop, there appeared to be an increase in political corruption. Economic decline seemed rampant. The second Stuart king, Charles I, began in 1625 to implement policies that diminished the independence of villages like Groton. Under the king's authority, the archbishop of Canterbury began to interfere with the local churches, including those like Winthrop's that were managed and funded by the local manor lord.

In 1629, Winthrop sold his village and joined with a network of Puritan friends, many of them connected through Cambridge University, in purchasing stock in the Massachusetts Bay Company. Winthrop set sail aboard the *Arbella* and reached Salem in June 1630. As the stockholders of a company to set up a community in America, Winthrop and his friends regained an extensive amount of economic, political, and religious independence. Although villages in England were losing their autonomy under Charles I's policy of political and religious centralization, company charters to America did not receive the same close oversight.

The stockholders elected the forty-one-year-old Winthrop their governor. Hundreds of farmers and trades people joined the expedition as workers—many of them people who had previously rented from or worked for the stockholders. At this time Winthrop composed his "Model of Christian Charity." Although much would later be said about the motivation for religious freedom that spurred the Puritans to this moment, the essay itself is just as much about politics, economics, and specifically the need to reclaim local autonomy and responsibility against the centralizing tendency of the king.

The greatness of Winthrop's essay, and the Puritan migration in general, is that, though Winthrop and the Puritans sought to regain lost freedom, they succeeded in doing so much more with the freedom they gained than they ever would have been able to do in England even if they had never lost their Elizabethan freedom. The call of Winthrop's words and the actions he led in Massachusetts far exceeded any selfish attempt of a threatened owner of a village to gain control of a new village.

The conclusion of "A Model of Christian Charity" is the most important part of Winthrop's essay. "It rests now to make some application," he declared. First, those who claim to be Christians should be "knit together" in a "bond of Love." Second, church and town governments must work together and the public good must "oversway all private respects." Third, the goal is "to improve our lives, to do more service to the Lord." Fourth, and most significantly, "Whatsoever we did or ought to have done when we lived in England, the same must we do and more also where we go."

Winthrop declared a contract between the Puritans and God. God has "ratified" the contract and further commissioned the Puritans to get to work. God, Winthrop threatened, "will expect strict performance." Given this threat, there is only one way to success: "to do justly, to love mercy, to walk humbly with our God."

It is in this context that Winthrop then closes with the "city upon a hill" line. But note that the line is in the context of failure not success:

> For we must consider that we shall be as a City upon a Hill, the eyes of all people are upon us; so that if we shall deal falsely with our God in this work we have undertaken, and so cause Him to withdraw His present help from us, we shall be a by-word through the world.

With such a speech about such a contract and such a commission, how could anyone expect Winthrop and the Puritans to succeed? In fact, they did not succeed—in the long run. In his own diary, Winthrop reported the frustrations and failures. "As the people increased," he wrote twelve years after arriving in New England, "so sin abounded."

But early on, Winthrop and his company made an heroic effort to succeed. The story of the initial implementation of Winthrop's speech makes it amazing that he did succeed. Winthrop turned his directorship into an annually elected position. Voting was extended more widely among the people than ever before in England. Renters became land-owners. Rich people took less than what they could have demanded. Local government was given autonomy. Ministers restrained their political power. Public education was ensured to all children. Virtuous economics was encouraged and price-gouging punished. Surely anyone watching had to admit that the Puritans used their increased freedom to do more political, economic, and religious good in America than was ever possible in England

Take first the change in Winthrop's position from company director to governor and the extension of voting rights. The stockholders of the Massachusetts Bay Company were a relatively small number of men who were given extensive powers to run their business. Winthrop was elected director by these stockholders. Normal expectation would have the on-site stockholders set up shop in America as an all-powerful aristocracy. Communities of utopian dreamers tend to centralize power rather than disperse it. Winthrop and the stockholders, however, began almost immediately to reinterpret their royal charter so as to set up a little Puritan republic rather than the business venture that it legally was.

On October 19, 1630, Winthrop and seven stockholders met in an open meeting, as Edmund Morgan writes, to implement "a revolution that was to affect the history of Massachusetts from that time forward" (Morgan, p. 90). Essentially, ownership was extended out to "the people"—that vague term that at that time meant most of the adult males in Massachusetts. What used to be a company was now a self-governing commonwealth with "the people" having the power to elect a legislature, which, in turn, had the power to appoint yearly a governor and deputy governor.

The only way to understand such a move is to see that Winthrop and his colleagues were serious about what was said in "A Model of Christian Charity." If the Puritans were supposed to be "knit together" with everybody responsible for the success or failure of the enterprise, then

Winthrop and the stockholders had to share responsibility and control with those who had not initially put up any money.

Next, consider the fact that renters became landowners and rich people willingly took less than they might have. When migrating to America, a large number of small farmers and townspeople joined the endeavor. Although many of these people had sold their land in England and were prepared to buy in America, there were also many people who had not owned any land. Many farmers in England held long-term leases from men like Winthrop who, we must remember, owned the whole village of Groton and the surrounding farms. Winthrop could have easily expected a similar deal for himself in America, expecting the poorer immigrants to rent land from him and the other company owners. Even the Quaker William Penn, famous for being nice to Indians and religiously tolerant, held on to his legal right of landownership when he and the Quakers came to Pennsylvania in the 1680s. Penn and his family required a "quitrent" from colonists for the use of the land. Penn also built for himself a mansion on a large estate outside his "city of brotherly love."

Winthrop and his fellow stockholders never tried to rent land. They encouraged land ownership. Land was given away, free, to immigrants. Former renters and poor tradespeople received a town lot upon which to build a house and a field lot upon which to farm. Winthrop built himself a nice house, but certainly no mansion. He lived on a town lot in Boston. None of the original stockholders demanded a huge estate in return for their investment.

We must understand that Winthrop and the Puritans were not egalitarian, but they did believe in community responsibility. Winthrop's "Model of Christian Charity" begins with the simple distinction that there are two ranks of people: the rich and the poor. When giving out land, the Puritans tended to give the people who had been richer in England a little more than the formerly landless. The Puritans did not want to undermine social distinctions. Responsibility was what they were after, not equality. In his speech, Winthrop offered several biblical precedents for "enlargement towards others, and less respect towards our selves and our own right."

Here again, we must see the reality behind the rhetoric of Winthrop's call to do "whatsoever we did or ought to have done when we lived in England, the same must we do and more also where we go." Only this way could the Puritans "improve our lives, to do more service to the Lord." Winthrop wanted everyone in Massachusetts to start "rich" and not "poor." Being "rich" he defined not by estate and servants, rather by the ability "to live comfortably by their own means." The Puritan contract with God needed everyone to have such basic comfort so that they could be "knit together" and spend their days improving Massachusetts instead of worrying about subsistence.

Next in the list of applications rooted in Winthrop's "Model of Christian Charity" is the encouragement of local autonomy and the restraint of ministerial power. The English people had a long history of believing their freedom was rooted in local autonomy. A well-functioning England depended not on centralized authority but on well-functioning parts making up the whole. In the book of I Corinthians, Paul had advocated a view of the church as different body parts working together as a whole. The Puritans had much to draw from when thinking of autonomous parts making up strong wholes. Winthrop in his speech said it this way: "There is no body but consists of parts, and that which knits these parts together gives the body perfection."

For the Puritans, Massachusetts must consist of multilayered covenants. The marriage covenant was the root of a family covenant, which was the root of church, and town covenants, which were the blossoms in the bouquet of Massachusetts Bay Colony's convenant with God. The whole needed the parts to function well. No king or bishop at the center could make society function well, only the autonomous parts could make the whole work. There was, therefore, much emphasis on independent towns and churches. In fact, people were not allowed to live alone either as individuals or families. Nobody was given land unless they were part of a family covenant, and the family had to live on a town lot. Unmarried men were thought to be dangerous. People without responsibilities to other people were hard to knit into the fabric of society. Families had to be knit together with other families. A family living out on a farm, far from other families, was useless in building a city on a hill. Families must be gathered together in towns and churches. Only then could everybody watch over everybody else. Wife-beaters could be revealed, sick mothers could be helped with their children, and barns could be raised. Talented children could be identified, and patrons could be organized to send them to college. Only in a town and church could sinners be punished, and the saints encouraged.

So when immigrants arrived they were told to organize themselves into towns and form churches before they were allotted land. Every town had to have a minister, and ministers had to be educated. Many ministers were part of the Cambridge University Puritan network. It would have been easy to have given the ministers special power in the towns, but that was not the Puritan way. The ministers actually encouraged a restriction of their power. Puritans believed in separation of church and state. Roman Catholics and Anglicans mixed their clergy and government bureaucracy so much that the Puritans believed this helped cause impurity in both church and state. The Puritans like to call themselves a "New English Israel," which to them indicated a strict differentiation between the role of magistrate and minister. In Winthrop's speech he delineated two types of law: Moral Law and the Law of the Gospel. The two must work together in society, but they were divided into the separate realms of state and church.

Where church and state connected in Puritan Massachusetts was in town government and with the voters. Only church members in good standing could vote. This was the crucial link between the highest Christian ideals of the colony and its political structure. The link was not at the top of the pyramid of government but at the base. Church membership was based on a declaration of one's experience of Christ's mercy and a recognition of one's sinfulness.

The whole structure and purpose of the Massachusetts Bay Colony rested on the vitality of towns and churches—and especially the education that towns and churches were supposed to supply. Within the first decade in America, the Puritans passed laws requiring towns to supply public education for Bible literacy, and Harvard College was created to grow a crop of highly educated Puritan leaders. The educated ministers in the towns usually took the responsibility of teaching Latin and Greek to college-bound boys.

Not all towns were able to keep schools at all times, but the Puritans never lost their passion for the connection of politics, religion, and education. Whenever Puritan vitality seemed to be waning, colonial leaders took up the call for increased education. Cotton Mather reminisced about "the ardour with which I once heard" a minister pray at one of their regional clergy gatherings: "Lord, for schools every where among us! That our schools may flourish! That every member of this assembly may go home and procure a good school to be encouraged in the town where he lives!" Winthrop's "Model of Christian Charity" says nothing directly about education, but its rational structure and reliance on biblical and legal assumptions leaves no doubt that he expected education to be the foundation of the social model he was describing.

With respect to economics, Winthrop advocated a virtuous business world that condemned pricing anything by what the market will bear.

He had no vision of a capitalistic system of individuals working for their own benefit. "The care of the public," he declared, "must oversway all private respects." The goal certainly was "to improve our lives," but only for the purpose of doing "more service to the Lord."

In 1639, Winthrop as governor had to face capitalism in the ideas of a Christian merchant named Robert Keayne who was fined by the legislature for overcharging. Merchants were supposed to profit according to their level of wit and energy but not at the expense of the community fairness. Winthrop recorded in his diary a sermon on false economic principles given soon after by a Boston minister:

> Some false principles were these:—
> 1. That a man might sell as dear as he can, and buy as cheap as he can.
> 2. If a man lose by casualty of sea, etc. in some of his commodities, he may raise the price of the rest.
> 3. That he may sell as he bought, though he paid too dear, etc. and though the commodity be fallen, etc.
> 4. That as a man may take the advantage of his own skill or ability, so he may of another's ignorance or necessity.

The city on a hill as preached in "A Model of Christian Charity" was not a utopia. Utopias usually depend on the belief that human nature is good and that a bad environment is what keeps most societies from attaining purity. The Puritan city on a hill was a republic of Christian voters gathered in towns and churches where individual sinfulness could be inhibited by peer pressure. Puritans believed in the inherent sinfulness of individuals and had no illusions about their colony attaining purity.

Using the language of later founding fathers, Winthrop wanted to create a "more perfect" society. As he said in the speech, he wanted to take the politics, religion, and economics of village life in England and make it better. The end product would be a model to the world.

An often-stated irony about the Puritans is that they wanted religious toleration for themselves but refused to extend it to others. While this is superficially true, we should recognize that Winthrop's speech never said anything about religious liberty or toleration. Winthrop's speech was about knitting together people into a web of politics, religion, and economics with underlying assumptions about education. The Puritan creation of a loose republic rooted in independent towns and churches established the web. Those who refused to fully participate in the web were punished in much the same way English towns punished those unwilling to abide by the social contract.

In 1680, more than a half-century after the founding of the colony, England imposed religious toleration on Massachusetts and demanded that voting no longer be restricted to church members. But the loose town and church structure of the commonwealth was becoming too loose anyway. Success was killing them. As Winthrop noted early: "As people increased, so sin abounded." Too many people wanted to come to the city upon a hill, thus turning it into nothing more than a dynamic English colony. When English imperial policy demanded a break between church membership and the right to vote, the key innovation of the city upon a hill was destroyed. What was left was just the shell of Winthop's model.

But even the shell of the plan has long been influential. By the time of Samuel and John Adams in the 1770s, towns remained the most powerful force in Massachusetts politics. Calling a "town meeting" is still a catchphrase of participatory democracy. A good case could be made today that it is not Winthrop's speech that is important in American history; rather, it is simply the line about being a city upon a hill. That our town-based, participatory democracy should be exported to the rest of the world.

On the other hand, the deep ideas contained in the "Model of Christian Charity" and their implementation in colonial Massachusetts are inspiring. John Winthrop and his fellow stockholders led one of the greatest events in American history. A small band of rich Protestant men voluntarily diminished their own power in order to launch a social experiment they hoped would inspire the world.

SELECTED BIBLIOGRAPHY

Axtell, James. *The Invasion Within: The Contest of Cultures in Colonial North America*. New York: Oxford University Press, 1985. This study of Indian, French, and British contact emphasizes how New France's better relations with Indians long made up for the problem of a few French colonists.

Bailyn, Bernard. *The Peopling of British North America: An Introduction*. New York: Knopf, 1986. Probably the most important historian of colonial America of the generation after Edmund S. Morgan, Bailyn does not emphasize the role of towns. This book, however, is an overview of the immigration patterns that served to fill the towns of America.

Bradford, William. *Of Plymouth Plantation, 1620–1647*. Edited by Samuel Eliot Morison. New York: The Modern Library, 1967. Bradford, a governor of

Plymouth Colony, wrote this very readable history of his colony's early years.

Breen, T. H. *Puritans and Adventurers: Change and Persistence in Early America*. New York: Oxford University Press, 1980. An excellent collection of essays comparing Northern and Southern town life, government, and immigration.

Bridenbaugh, Carl. *Cities in the Wilderness: The First Century of Urban Life in America, 1625–1742*. New York: Oxford University Press, 1938. A Fundamental study of town life in British America.

Dawson, Hugh J. "John Winthrop's Rite of Passage: The Origins of the 'Christian Charitie' Discourse," *Early American Literature* 26 (1991): 219–231. Dawson argues that Winthrop wrote and delivered his speech before leaving land in England. The oldest testimony to the speech, however, says it was written on board the *Arbella*.

Fischer, David Hackett. *Albion's Seed: Four British Folkways in America*. New York: Oxford University Press, 1989. Fischer analyzes folkways that manifest the deep social connection between Britain and her colonies.

Fries, Sylvia Doughty. *The Urban Ideal in Colonial America*. Philadelphia: Temple University Press, 1977. Fries emphasizes the ideals involved in founding Boston, New Haven, Philadelphia, Williamsburg, and Savannah.

Goodwin, Rutherfoord. *A Brief & True Report concerning Williamsburg in Virginia*. Williamsburg: Colonial Williamsburg Inc., 1941. A good study of the founding.

Lockridge, Kenneth A. *A New England Town: The First Hundred Years*. New York: W. W. Norton, 1970. Lockridge builds up the utopianism of the Puritan settlement ideal so that he can then emphasize the fall. Powell's *Puritan Village* is better because it has less of an axe to grind, but both are key studies of the intricacy of a seventeenth-century town.

Mather, Cotton. *Magnalia Christi Americana*. First published in London in 1702. Anonymously edited with translations in 1853 and reproduced in Carlisle, PA: Banner of Truth, 1979. Any serious student of Colonial New England must read Mather's history.

Morgan, Edmund S. *The Puritan Dilemma: The Story of John Winthrop*. Boston: Little, Brown, 1958. This classic studies the Puritan govenor's dilemma of how to separate without separating, how to be exclusive without being exclusive, and how to lead while encouraging self-government.

———. *American Slavery American Freedom: The Ordeal of Colonial Virginia*. New York: W. W. Norton, 1975. This classic work emphasizes the British idealism of the Virginia Company and the work of Edwin Sandys.

Morison, Samuel E. *Samuel de Champlain: Father of New France*. Boston: Little, Brown, 1972. Champlain, the founder of Quebec, did as much as he could to encourage stable town life in New France.

Powell, Sumner Chilton. *Puritan Village: The Formation of a New England Town*. Middletown, CT: Wesleyan University Press, 1963. In this Pulitzer Prize winning study Powell thoroughly discusses English town ideals.

Smith, John. *Captain John Smith: A Select Edition of His Writings*. Edited by Karen

Ordahl Kupperman. Williamsburg, VA: Institute of Early American History and Culture and Chapel Hill: University of North Carolina Press, 1988. An excellent short collection of Smith's writings, divided into categories of autobiography, Jamestown, relations with Indians, and relation to the environment.

Winthrop, John. *The Journal of John Winthrop, 1630–1649*. Edited by Richard S. Dunn and Laetitia Yeandle. Cambridge: Harvard University Press, 1996. A recent abridged edition of Winthrop's own view of the founding years.

The Pilgrims were idealized and romanticized in early American history, as this nineteenth-century illustration shows. (Reproduced from the Collections of the Library of Congress.)

5

Early European–Native American Encounters, 1607–1637

INTRODUCTION

The English who first colonized North America received their earliest perceptions about American Indians, or Native Americans, from the Spanish, who, with the exception of Bartolomé de las Casas (infrequently read in England), characterized the Natives in the most unflattering terms. The first book in English on America was seen in 1511, and it described Indians as "lyke beasts without any resonablenes. . . . And they ete also on[e] another, the man ete his wyf his children. . . . They hange also the bodyes or persons fleshe in the smoke as men do with us swynes fleshe" (quoted in Stannard, p. 226).

To philosophers and intellectuals of the day, such people were barely human; indeed, some believed them to be satanic progeny of a human-animal coupling. Thus the vast majority of Englishmen came to North America predisposed to treat Indians with undisguised hostility. As Robert Gray, an early Virginia settler, put it in 1609, "[They are] incredibly rude, they worship the divell, offer their young children in sacrifice to him, wander up and down like beasts, and in manners and conditions, differ very little from beasts" (quoted in Stannard, p. 227).

By the late sixteenth century, most Europeans had concluded that Indians probably were human, but that they were still godless and lawless.

English treatment of Indians worsened as the colonial experiment wore on and settlers saw that the Natives were not going to submit either to their religion or their laws. For them to reject those basic tenets of English culture meant that they must be "less than rational and thus less than human" (Stannard, p. 229).

The English colonists simply had difficulty accepting Indians for what they were; they were too conscious of the racial differences and as a consequence, instinctively antagonistic. As the interpretive essay for this chapter points out, there were exceptions. Thomas Mayhew got along well with the Indians on Martha's Vineyard for many years. John Eliot spent fifteen years learning the Algonquin language and then translating the Bible into Algonquin before going out to do missionary work among the Indians. After thirty years, he claimed 1,500 "praying Indians" and another 1,000 converted Natives living in special villages throughout the Plymouth Colony.

Much of the European concern for Indians involved a desire to convert them to Christianity, as John Eliot spent much of life doing. But in general, the Church of England and its Puritan offspring did not make much of a concerted effort to win the souls of the Indians. Clergy were reluctant to do missionary work among the tribes when the pay was low and the conditions uncomfortable and occasionally dangerous. Most preferred the traditional life of serving a parish in a colonial town.

The French were better able to adapt to the Indians. Although the French Jesuit missionaries thought that the Natives were barbarians, they still wanted to convert them to Catholicism. Perhaps the Catholic faith appealed more to the Indians, or perhaps the Jesuits were better prepared for their task. They often knew the Indian dialect, for example, while Protestant missionaries seldom had any formal preparation.

On the other hand, Dutch relations with the Indians were strictly commercial. Early on in the Dutch colonial experience, perhaps around 1618, informal trade with the Mohawk Indians began. The Indians brought furs to the Dutch and in return received muskets at a rate of twenty beaver pelts for one gun. At first relatively few muskets fell into Indian hands by means of this trade, but by the 1640s, when French-English rivalry accelerated the pace of war, the Mohawks, part of the Iroquois federation, had acquired many more muskets. When the English replaced the Dutch as trading partners with the Indians, they too supplied guns for furs.

In general, Dutch relations with Indians were good since the beginning of their settlement. The colony of New Netherland grew quite slowly and thus was less threatening to the Indians than the rapidly expanding English colonies in New England. Before the 1620s, the Dutch were always careful to treat the Indians with dignity and pay them for their land. The Dutch West India Company stipulated that "everyone should be strict in dealing with the Indians—no one should give offense to their person, their womenfolk, or their possessions" (quoted in Edmonds, p. 168).

By the late 1620s, this attitude was changing. The Indians were less in awe of the Dutch, who began to consider the Indians a nuisance. Jonas Michaelius, one of the first pastors to come to New Netherland, thought that the Indians were "stupid as posts, proficient in all wickedness and godlessness . . . thievish and treacherous as they are tall" (quoted in Edmonds, p. 168). Perhaps this is why Dutch-Indian relations were strictly commercial.

The first phase of English–Native American relations ended with the brutal Pequot War of 1637. The Pequots were a Connecticut tribe that before the 1630s had had little contact with either the English or the Dutch. They had been involved in fighting other nearby tribes, but they did not perceive the English or the Dutch as threats to their security or territory.

Indian-white distrust in New England began in 1615, even before the first permanent settlement, when an English sea captain, Thomas Hunt, captured fifteen Indians while loading fish and sold them to the Spanish as slaves. Out of this group came Squanto, educated and converted by the Jesuits and a friend later to the English. Prior to Squanto's return in the early 1620s, however, word of the kidnapping spread among different Indian groups, and when a smallpox epidemic accompanied the rumors, killing many natives, the Indians could not have viewed the white people in a favorable light. The English, on the other hand, saw the epidemic as a mark of God's favor.

The Pequots were not affected by the smallpox epidemic; at that time, they were still too isolated from contact with Europeans. After the English began coming to New England in the 1620s, they did have occasion to deal with the newcomers, and they were considered peaceful and honorable in those dealings. Described as "stately and warlike," they were known to engage in wars with their Indians neighbors, such as the Mohawks.

Trouble between the English and the Pequots began in 1633 when a renegade band of Pequots killed a trading party led by Captain John Stone, something of a renegade himself and a person whose immoral behavior had cause the Massachusetts Bay Colony authorities to expel him on two separate occasions. Sassacus, the Pequot chief, was concerned enough about this incident to send a delegation to Boston to seek a treaty of friendship with the English. The Indians succeeded in convincing the colonists that there had been no profit to them for the deed; indeed eight of the ten Indians involved had soon after died of smallpox. The Pequots agreed to turn over the two surviving attackers, but they never did.

Nonetheless, the incident was apparently forgotten, and there was a period of calm until 1636, when another incident, even worse than the John Stone affair, took place near Block Island, off the Connecticut coast. A ship belonging to John Oldham was seen adrift, with Indians on deck, who fled when a ship commanded by John Gallup approached. Gallup's ship rammed Oldham's and several Indians who had not previously fled jumped (or fell) overboard and drowned. Gallup boarded Oldham's ship, found two more Indians and took them prisoner, and then found Oldham's body, his head, hands, and feet cut off. In addition, most of the cargo was missing.

Massachusetts Bay Colony governor Henry Vane learned that several Indians who had managed to escape from Oldham's ship had gone to the Pequots, who were apparently protecting them. Vane sent a delegation to the Pequots, who surrendered two boys who had been members of Oldham's crew and promised to return the stolen cargo. The Indians evidently felt that this was a reasonable compromise, but the colonists were not satisfied. There were a few minor skirmishes over the matter, but the violence was minimal.

After a difficult winter in 1636–37, marked by Pequot raids on colonial settlements and the kidnapping of two teenaged girls, who were later released unhurt, New England leaders decided that the Pequots had to be eliminated, and a force of ninety colonists and seventy Mohegan Indians (enemies of the Pequot) set out for Pequot territory. They were later joined by an indeterminate number of Narragansetts, who were also enemies of the Pequots. The combined force managed to approach a sizable Pequot town without detection and attacked late at night, setting the town afire and firing musket volleys at Indians trying to flee. By dawn, the town was in ashes and all but fourteen of the 700 Pequots who had lived there were dead. A month later, another English force invaded Pequot country and killed several hundred more Indians. When the Mohawks killed Sassacus, who had fled to them for protection, the war, such as it was, ended, and the Pequot nation was dead. Most English settlers saw the whole affair as another indication of God's working his will.

If English muskets failed to kill Indians, their diseases made up for it. As in the Spanish world, European diseases proved fatal to thousands of Indians in the early years of colonization in New England. A smallpox epidemic in 1616–17, apparently brought by fishing vessels trading with Indians, killed enough Natives to eliminate them as a major threat to the Plymouth Colony after 1620. Smallpox continued to be a health problem in the 1630s, killing substantial numbers of settlers but many more Indians. A major epidemic in 1639–40 in the St. Lawrence River valley and nearby areas killed many Huron Indians, reducing that tribe's population to ten thousand from the twenty to thirty-five thousand it had been at the beginning of the century. The Iroquois were similarly decimated in the 1660s.

The English could have quarantined smallpox patients and made an effort to reduce the spread of the disease, as the Spanish and Portuguese tried to do (though without great success). But the English were not concerned with the physical well-being of the Indians and, indeed, welcomed what they considered an obvious manifestation of God's blessings upon them.

INTERPRETIVE ESSAY
Kathleen Perdisatt and Rick Kennedy

Seventeenth-century North American history is the story of a contest for domination. In that contest, the Native Americans ultimately lost and British culture won. The greatest failure in seventeenth-century America was the inability of Natives and the settlers to construct a mutually beneficial life together in North America. From the grand perspective of the history of our nation it is appropriate to emphasize the tragic and doomed battles of the Indians against dispossession as European disease, population growth, and land-grabbing proved unstoppable. Within the largely tragic story, however, there are many small stories of creative people trying to work against the tide. In the seventeenth century, Pocahontas, Squanto, and Hiacoomes, along with settlers in the regions surrounding Jamestown, Virginia, and Cape Cod, Massachusetts, tried to create the biracial relationship that might have undercut the beginnings of the contest for domination.

Pocahontas was a young woman who aspired to do what Americans throughout history have never been able to do: create productive cross-cultural relations between Native and non-Native Americans. Pocahontas was the daughter of Wahunsonacock, who also went by the name Powhatan. Wahunsonacock was the dynamic emperor of eastern Virginia. He ruled thirty separate tribes that were together called the Powhatans. Pocahontas was a favored daughter who shared her father's vivacity and leadership abilities.

With the founding of Jamestown by the British in 1607, misunderstandings and distrust abounded. Wahunsonacock apparently thought that the English with their guns and technology could be useful to Powhatan imperial expansion. On the English side, the unruly but talented John Smith was sure he was dealing with savages who could not be trusted. He and his fellow English invaders were much too suspicious of the surrounding Indians to think much about what they were doing and what was happening.

Edmund S. Morgan calls the British situation in Jamestown a "fiasco" of organization and direction. Wahunsonacock and the Powhatans willingly supplied Jamestown with food and help; but Smith, distrustful of this arrangement, tells us that he would come armed to get these gifts. Smith reported that in one encounter Wahunsonacock told him that he need not bring weapons "for here they are needlesse we being friends." Smith refused to believe the chief and, shortly after, even pointed his gun at and demanded supplies from Opechancanough, the king's brother and eventual successor. Opechancanough was already opposed to his brother's way of handling the British, and Smith succeeded only in justifying Opechancanough's own paranoia.

The climate of distrust continued when, in 1608, Smith was "captured" by the Powhatans. Smith described his situation:

> A long consultation was held, but the conclusion was, two great stones were brought before [Wahunsonacock]: then as many as could lay hands on [me], dragged [me] to them, and thereon laid [my] head, and being ready with their clubs, to beate out [my] braines, Pocahontas the Kings dearest daughter, when no intreaty could prevaile, got [my] head in her

armes, and laid her owne upon [mine] to save [me] from death: whereat the Emperour was contented [I] should live.

Two days later, Wahunsonacock, ceremonially dressed in imperial garb, came to Smith and "told him now they were friends," and sent him back to Jamestown.

Smith thought that Pocahontas had saved his life and that her tricky father had some plan up his sleeve. In truth, we do not know what really happened; however, it appears that John Smith had not been a prisoner but an honored—if coerced—guest. The Powhatan emperor had ceremoniously inducted Smith and Jamestown into his empire. John Smith, after a ceremony of submission, was now a subchief of the Powhatans and sent back to his people. Pocahontas, an eleven- or twelve-year-old girl at that time, was either playing a role in the ceremony or trying to calm Smith.

Pocahontas was also at the center of another confusion: Wahunsonacock's coronation as a subject-king under the king of England. Smith tells us that after Wahunsonacock was asked to come to Jamestown, some English soldiers were surprised by a "hydeous noise" coming from the woods. Smith and the colonists grabbed their guns thinking the natives were attacking, "but presently Pocahontas came, willing him to kill her if any hurt were intended." Pocahontas then joined with thirty other young women in a dance. The next day Wahunsonacock arrived. The colonists attempted to explain what was happening and the emperor did not readily participate. "Foule trouble there was to make him kneele to receive his Crowne," Smith wrote.

In the midst of two coerced ceremonies of subjection was a young girl who may have understood the big picture better than either her father or Smith. As the Powhatans and the British vied ceremonially to make each the subchief of the other, Pocahontas played the role of mediator. Many children's stories and cartoons have completely distorted the story of Pocahontas; however, they usually have the main point right. Pocahontas, the loving and fearless child, represents the possibility of a relationship of trust between the invaders and the ruling empire.

Between 1608 and 1610, Pocahontas was a welcome visitor in Jamestown, often carrying messages to and from her father. Smith and other leaders of Jamestown had sown much distrust but young Pocahontas was oblivious to the danger. In 1610, however, war broke out between Powhatans and the colonists, and in 1613 the colonists captured Pocahontas and brought her to Jamestown. She became a diplomatic hostage but does not seem to have thought of herself as a hostage. She freely converted to Christianity and consented to marry John Rolfe in 1614. She may have helped Rolfe and the English learn to grow tobacco during this time. Wahunsonacock consented to the marriage, which brought the war to an end.

Pocahontas apparently loved Rolfe. She could have escaped. Eventually she bore a child who became a symbol for the possibility of mutually beneficial biracial relations. Pocahontas and Rolfe agreed to sail to England to publicize the possibility of peace, but sadly, Pocahontas died in England in 1617 from a European disease. Many people have written about Pocahontas as a victim sacrificed to a British farce. But this is too cynical. The British had high hopes of bringing peace to the fiasco in Jamestown, and Pocahontas's marriage and child symbolized the best possibility. She seems to have willingly embraced the people of Jamestown and accepted the role of peacemaker between the English and her people. She died pursuing her aspiration.

Her father died two years later, leaving Opechancanough to spread his distrust. The relationship between Opechancanough and Smith, not Pocahontas and Rolfe, became the model for seventeenth-century Virginia. In March 1622, Opechancanough orchestrated widespread attacks on English settlements. The attacks, however, did not stop immigration and only encouraged distrust.

Business relationships between the Indians and the British in Virginia continued throughout the seventeenth century; however, hope for sharing the land, intermarriage, and raising mixed-blood children was gone. By the 1670s, the Natives had been pushed across the Blue Ridge Mountains. British settlers on the Virginia frontier for the rest of the century fueled more hatred and distrust in ongoing skirmishes.

Assimilation was the term eventually adopted in the eighteenth century as the answer the "the Indian problem." By then assimilation clearly meant the destruction of the weaker culture in favor of the adoption of the stronger. In the seventeenth century, assimilation still could have meant something more benign and mutually beneficial. Pocahontas hoped for this type of assimilation. Squanto (also known as Tisquantum), the Patuxet who taught the Pilgrims to fertilize their corn with fish, also aspired to assimilate natives and non-natives into a mutually beneficial relationship.

Squanto was a highly intelligent and versatile native of Patuxet, a thriving town of some two thousand people on what is now Plymouth Bay, Massachusetts. At the time of Jamestown's founding (1607), Patuxet and other coastal New England towns were developing a trading relationship with European ships fishing for cod. John Smith, after leaving Jamestown in 1608, sailed to Cape Cod in 1614 and gave the region the name New England. A companion ship with Smith was captained by a man who wanted to make some extra money by capturing some Indians to sell as slaves in Spain. Squanto and twenty other Wampanoags from Patuxet were lured on board and placed in chains.

A Spanish priest later freed Squanto, but finding himself now in Europe Squanto began learning what he could from the Europeans while working toward getting home. Not much is known about his travels in Europe, but we know that after three years he was living in London, helping prospective colonists and explorers with information about New England. Five years after leaving America, he found a chance to go back by sailing with a colonizing mission. The mission failed, but Squanto returned home in 1619.

However, New England had been ravaged by European diseases while Squanto was away. The Bostonian Cotton Mather would later write that God had "wonderfully prepared" the New World for Puritan "entertainment, by a sweeping mortality that had lately been among the natives." Mather wrote that only one-tenth, even one-twentieth, of the natives remained "so that the woods were almost cleared of those pernicious creatures, to make room for a better growth." William Bradford, one of the founding Pilgrims of Plymouth Colony, was more respectful of what he called "the late great mortality." Bradford reported that "skulls and bones were found in many places lying still above the ground where their houses and dwellings had been, a very sad spectacle to behold." Such was the spectacle Squanto beheld upon his return. But again, Squanto did not fall into despair.

When Bradford and the Pilgrims arrived at Squanto's hometown in 1620 they were understandably fearful of Indian attack. Initially the Natives kept their distance except for stealing some tools. On March 16, an Indian from the north named Samoset who spoke broken English walked out of the woods to greet the English. Samoset later returned with several local Wampanoags carrying the Pilgrims' stolen goods. With the Wampanoags was Squanto and their *sachem* (Indian chief) Massasoit. After some "friendly entertainments," the Pilgrims and the Wampanoags then negotiated a long-lasting peace agreement:

1. That neither he nor any of his should injure or do hurt to any of their people.

2. That if any of his did hurt to any of theirs, he should send the offender, that they might punish him.

3. That if anything were taken away from any of theirs, he should cause it to be restored; and they should do the like to his.

4. If any did unjustly war against him, they would aid him; if any did war against them, he should aid them.

5. He should send to his neighbours confederates to certify them of this, that they might not wrong them, but might be likewise comprised in the conditions of peace.

6. That when their men came to them, they should leave their bows and arrows behind them. (Bartett, p. 188)

Governor Bradford described Squanto as "a special instrument sent of God for their good beyond their expectation." He was the intermediary of the peace treaty and chose to settle with the English. His teaching the Pilgrims to grow corn is one of the great traditions of American education. He was the key figure in making possible the first Thanksgiving celebration when Massasoit and ninety Wampanoags joined the Pilgrims for three days of happy feasting. Squanto spent most of his time brokering deals between various tribes and the English. He died of an "Indian fever" in 1622 on a trading mission helping Miles Standish. In his last days, Squanto gave gifts to his English friends and "remembrances of his love."

Squanto, after the loss of his own town, was able to embrace both the natives and the non-natives of Plymouth Bay. He was by far the most well-traveled, broadly experienced, linguistically versatile person in New England. Cynics have disparaged him as weak, but fail to give Squanto the credit he deserves. He was a townless Indian who seems to have been able to see beyond the tribal distrust and animosities of other natives and non-natives.

At one point Squanto seems to have made an attempt at centralizing power in himself as an intertribal leader. All we know of this story is William Bradford's version, which says Squanto told the Pakanokets to abandon Massasoit's leadership while, at the same time, encouraging the English to think Massasoit was going to betray them. Squanto, Bradford believed, was trying to undermine Massasoit's political position.

The story shows the complexity of Squanto's work brokering relations between local power centers. If Bradford's history is right, and Squanto was making a power-play for himself at that point, it raises the possibility that the person who had orchestrated the first peace treaty and Thanksgiving feast was attempting to do even greater good.

But Squanto did not gain an intertribal leadership position, and fifteen years after his death the Pequot War broke out. Governor Winthrop in Boston wrote to Governor Bradford in Plymouth: "we conceive that you look at the Pequots and all other Indians as a common enemy." Thirty years later, Massasoit's son, Metacom, believed the leaders of Plymouth Colony poisoned his brother. He and the English no longer upheld the treaty written with Squanto's help. In the 1670s Metacom galvanized Indian resistance to the English and died in New England's most devastating civil war.

Pocahontas and Squanto died just at the point they might have done something great for relations between natives and non-natives. Maybe it is significant that both were "outsiders" in the sense that one was a girl and young woman—a weak position in foreign affairs—and the other was homeless. Hiacoomes was also an outsider, but he did not die young. His story, along with that of the Mayhew family, represents the best hope in the seventeenth century for a mutually beneficial relationship between the British and the Indians.

Hiacoomes and the Mayhew family were the most influential people on the island of Martha's Vineyard. In 1641, Thomas Mayhew, Sr. became, in the presumptuous fashion of the English, the "owner" and governor of Nantucket and Martha's Vineyard, which are islands near the southern coast of Cape Cod. The island Indians were Wampanoags related to those under Massasoit rule on the mainland. The native government of Martha's Vineyard, the larger island, was hierarchical with four *sachems* ruling separate districts. Mayhew, breaking from the Puritan tradition and not wanting to fall fully into the presumptuous land-grabbing of the English, insisted on "purchasing" land from the natives as he began the process of encouraging British colonization.

In 1643, Thomas Mayhew, Jr., son of the governor, moved onto the island with his family as a farmer and missionary. The younger Mayhew had learned to speak the Algonquian dialect of the Wampanoags and hoped to create Puritan towns where Indians and British Christians could live together.

Hiacoomes was Mayhew's first convert. Hiacoomes was somewhat of an outcast from the Wampanoag community and was open to the Christian gospel. Beginning in 1643 Mayhew trained Hiacoomes as a comissionary working toward the creation of a church and covenanted Christian town. Given the relative strength of the Native culture on the island and the weakness of the Mayhews, there was no extreme pressure for Indians to convert; however, many Indians eventually converted, founded, or joined churches, and moved into "praying towns." After an epidemic in 1645 a large number of Indians came to Hiacoomes "to be instructed by him; and some Persons of Quality, such as before had despised him, sent for him to come and instruct them."

By 1651, Hiacoomes was the co-minister of his own church of 199 professed believers. Sharing the leadership was Momonequem, one of Hiacoomes' converts. In 1652, the Wampanoags asked Thomas Mayhew, Jr., to draw up a town covenant similar to other Puritan town covenants. We are told "Mr. *Mayhew* drew up an excellent *Covenant* in their native Language, which he often read and made plain to them: and they all with free Consent and Thankfulness united in it, and desired the Grace and Help of GOD to keep it faithfully."

The mutually beneficial relationship of natives and non-natives that developed on Martha's Vineyard is best seen in the churches founded. From 1667 to 1684, there were no British clergy living on the island, only ordained Indian pastors. Natives and non-natives gathered in bilingual church services under the leadership of these Indian pastors for nearly two decades. Mayhew remembered from boyhood these church services and later reported to one of the ministers that the English "very chearfuly received the Lord's Supper from him."

The whole line of Mayhews on Martha's Vineyard from 1643–1806 should be remembered for the way they respected the rights of Indians. The Vineyard *sachems* had no desire to diminish their authority and let the British take over the island. From the beginning Thomas Mayhew, Sr., assured the *sachems* that the British had no desire to undermine their political jurisdiction and would respect the rights of any natives who chose not to become Christians. He assured them that "Religion and Government were distinct things." Throughout the seventeenth century, the natives were not dispossessed of their land or authority while Christian and non-Christian natives shared political power.

By the end of the seventeenth century six "praying towns" were established where Christian Wampanoags were encouraged to covenant together. Native towns, "praying towns," and Puritan towns existed peacefully together on the small island throughout the seventeenth century. Puritan political and religious theory was focused on the creation of towns with churches at the center. The Wampanoags of Martha's Vineyard had a similar focus on towns held together with deep religious commitments. In their situation of being isolated from the pressures of mainland British immigration, the Puritans and the Wampanoags developed a mode of appreciating each other. When in the 1670s Massasoits's son Metacom led the mainland Wampanoags into a brutal war against the Puritans, the Wampanoags of Martha's Vineyard refused to join and actually protected the British colonists on their island.

Hiacoomes and the Mayhews also joined in encouraging English education for whites and Indians. From 1650 to 1672 intellectually promising Indian boys were sent to grammar school on the mainland in order to learn the Latin and Greek required at Harvard College. Hiacoomes and Thomas Mayhew, Jr., sent their sons Joel and Matthew together to the Cambridge grammar school. Four other Wampanoags accompanied them. Sadly, two of these Indian boys died from British diseases contracted in the residential situation of the school. Diseases always flourish in the closed atmosphere of schools, and Indian mortality rates at schools were high in early America. In 1663, Joel, Matthew, and Caleb Cheshchaamog, the son of a Vineyard *sachem*, entered Harvard College, three of probably only five Indians to attend Harvard College in the seventeenth century. Tragically, Joel was murdered by some Indians on Nantucket Island just a few months before graduation. Caleb Cheshchaamog was the only native to graduate from Harvard in the seventeenth century.

Along with Hiacoomes' initial openness and long-term support, much credit should be given the Mayhew family who made the forging of an Indian-British community into a multigeneration family business. Thomas Mayhew, Jr., was recognized in his own day, along with mainlander John Eliot, as not only someone who "understood" the natives but also loved them. In 1658 he disappeared at sea, and his father, Thomas Mayhew, Sr., took up the responsibility of keeping the good relations and Christian hope going. More politically oriented, the elder Mayhew helped the Wampanoags reform their governing system, including instituting councils for conflict resolution and juries for criminal trials. The Mayhews continued to share leadership on the island with Wampanoag officials for over 150 years. By the time of the American Revolution most of the natives were Christians, but in the 1760s an epidemic ravaged the Wampanoag population. After the Revolution the natives were very weak and barely hung on to their past role on the island. Today, the island is a resort.

In the big picture of British-Indian relations, the stories of Pocahontas, Squanto, and Hiacoomes are only accounts of small and marginal successes. In all three stories there was a minimum requirement of religious toleration and openness. Certainly British Christians were always trying to convert Indians; however, John Smith, Governor Bradford, and the Mayhews did not limit good relations only to those who converted. Most importantly, in all three stories the natives and the settlers *wanted to get along* in the hope of some mutually beneficial end. Pocahontas, Squanto, and Hiacoomes *wanted* to construct something beneficial to all involved and persuaded John Rolfe, Governor Bradford, and the Mayhews to agree with them. All involved *wanted* peace.

Also Pocahontas, Squanto, and Hiacoomes were outsiders cut-off from the main lines of power. Pocahontas was a woman. Squanto had lost all family and community ties. Hiacoomes was not part of the hierarchical order of Martha's Vineyard. The Vineyard itself was an island cut off from the mainland and not subject to the same immigration pressures. Each Indian understood that greater opportunity and maybe even strength would come from developing relations with the British. As for the Englishmen most open to the Indians, John Rolfe needed a wife in a largely womanless community, Governor Bradford understood fully that his people could be easily massacred by Massasoit's warriors, and the Mayhews were owners of nearly worthless property who could not even keep a Puritan minister employed.

Perhaps mutually beneficial relations between peoples depends on weakness rather than strength. The stories of Pocahontas, Squanto, and Hiacoomes are indicators that in the seventeenth century a mutually beneficial relationship between the British and the Indians was possible. By the 1670s, however, the opportunity had passed.

SELECTED BIBLIOGRAPHY

Axtell, James. *The Invasion Within: The Contest of Cultures in Colonial North America*. New York: Oxford University Press, 1985. The most authoritative book on French, British, and Indian relations in the seventeenth century.

Banks, Charles Edward. *The History of Martha's Vineyard Dukes County Massachusetts in Three Volumes*. Edgartown, MA: Dukes County Historical Society, 1966. This extensive work on Martha's Vineyard includes several chapters dedicated to the missionary efforts of the Mayhew family and the history of the Native American population on the island.

Barbour, Philip L. *Pocahontas and Her World*. Boston: Houghton Mifflin, 1970. Presently the standard biography on Pocahontas. Primary documents relating to her are weak and leave a broad range of interpretation as to her character and motives. No one biography can be considered authoritative.

Bartlett, Robert M. *The Faith of the Pilgrims*. New York: United Church Press,

1978. Primarily a history of the Pilgrims' religious beliefs, this book also touches on their relationship with Indians.

Bradford, William. *Of Plymouth Plantation*. Edited by Samuel Eliot Morison. New York: Modern Library, 1952. The classic history. Virtually everything we know about Squanto comes from this book.

Edmonds, Walter D. *The Musket and the Cross*. Boston: Little, Brown, 1968. A study of the French and English struggle for North American colonial dominance.

Hauptman, Laurence M., and James D. Wherry, eds. *The Pequots in Southern New England: The Fall and Rise of an American Indian Nation*. Norman, OK: University of Oklahoma Press, 1990. The Pequot war shows the Puritans at their worst. Governor John Winthrop in Boston never felt the weakness of Governor Bradford, nor did he have the assistance of such a talented native as Squanto.

Jennings, Francis. *The Invasion of America: Indians, Colonialism, and the Cant of Conquest*. Chapel Hill, NC: University of North Carolina Press, 1975. As the title indicates, Jennings considers British rhetoric of desiring good relations with natives to be hypocritical. Although largely true, the book is overly cynical.

Johnson, Margery Ruth. *The Mayhew Mission to the Indians, 1643–1806*. Ann Arbor, MI: University Microfilms, 1976. Johnson's unpublished dissertation on the Mayhew family is the most exhaustive history of the family found in my research of the clan. Her use of extensive primary sources gives her writing authority.

Mather, Cotton. *Magnalia Christi Americana: or the Ecclesiastical History of New England*. Edited by Raymond J. Cunningham. New York: F. Ungar, 1970. Originally published in 1702, this history written close to the sources offers a biographical chapter on John Eliot, "The Apostle to the Indians." Eliot, who worked closely with the Mayhews, has always been more famous than the Mayhews because of this book.

Morgan, Edmund S. *American Slavery American Freedom: The Ordeal of Colonial Virginia*. New York: W.W. Norton, 1975. Very readable detailed account of the establishment of English settlements in Virginia during the seventeenth century.

Morrison, Dane. *A Praying People*. New York: Peter Lang, 1995. Morrison's work is a general text describing the work of Puritan missionaries in New England that focuses on the impact of missionaries on the native culture.

Rountree, Helen C. *The Powhatan Indians of Virginia: Their Traditional Culture*. Norman, OK: University of Oklahoma Press, 1989. This is the standard scholarly study of the Powhatans. The focus is on their own culture rather than relations with the British.

Salisbury, Neal. "Squanto: Last of the Patuxets." In *Struggle and Survival in Colonial America*. Edited by David G. Sweet and Gary B. Nash. Berkeley: University of California Press, 1981. This is an excellent short biography of the notable Native American.

Segal, Charles M., and David C. Stineback. *Puritans, Indians, and Manifest Destiny*.

New York: G. P. Putnam's Sons, 1977. The distinction of Segal and Stineback's book is its use of extensive quotations from primary sources.

Smith, John. *Captain John Smith: A Select Edition of His Writings*. Edited by Karen
Ordahl Kupperman. Williamsburg, VA and Chapel Hill, NC: Institute of
Early American History and Culture and the University of North Carolina
Press, 1988. Smith wrote of his adventures with the Powhatans in two
versions. Kupperman brings the two versions together and includes ex-
cellent footnotes.

Stannard, David. *American Holocaust*. New York: Oxford University Press, 1992.
A detailed history of the early encounters between Europeans and American Indians, with emphasis on the destructive effects of the diseases and
purposeful violence that the Europeans brought.

6

The Introduction of Slavery into North America, 1619

INTRODUCTION

From the beginning of African history, the diverse cultures of that continent practiced slavery, although it frequently was not based on racial differences. Cultures in Egypt, Greece, and Rome forced captives from wars into slavery without regard for race or ethnicity. As Muslims settled North Africa, they took African men and women as slaves and harem subjects and shipped others to Islamic lands in the Middle East. There, these slaves worked mainly as servants and were an indicator of their master's wealth and social position.

As W.E.B. Du Bois and John Hope Franklin have pointed out, the Renaissance gave Europeans the opportunity to break away from old customs and traditions and to search for ways to improve themselves both spiritually and physically. With this new freedom, however, there was no concomitant sense of social responsibility. To be free, one could justifiably take away the freedom of others. Along with this came the development of commerce-based economies founded on the accumulation of capital and the drive to exploit resources for purely economic gain. These resources came to include other human beings.

By the end of the 1300s, slaves were being brought from the west coast of Africa and sold in Europe. The Portuguese were the first to see the

The first Africans to come to North America as slaves arrived in Jamestown, Virginia in 1619. (Reproduced from the Collections of the Library of Congress.)

advantages of the slave trade, a practice that they and others occasionally justified as part of the struggle to win souls for Christ. They believed that a Christian slave, no matter how bad his or her lot, was better off than a heathen free person.

Europe, however, did not have much economic use for slaves. Most sectors of the European economies were not labor-intensive, and there was a surplus of white labor because of the enclosure movement, which limited farming opportunities.

Africans went to the Americas with the Spanish as early as 1501, fighting and working alongside their white colleagues. They also accompanied the French in some of their early explorations into what is now Canada and the Mississippi River valley. In neither case were the Africans considered to be slaves. It was different with the English. Africans did not come with them on their earliest exploration efforts to America.

When a need for a labor supply first became apparent, the Spanish enslaved indigenous Indians, to the great detriment of native societies, especially in the Caribbean. The combination of cruel treatment, disease, and the Indians' inability to adjust to the discipline demanded by their masters led to the deaths of thousands.

After the Indian experiment had failed, Europeans, and especially the English, looked to poor whites as the solution to their labor needs. In England, a common source of labor during the seventeenth century was indentured servitude. Typically, a person wishing to come to America would contract with a sponsor (or master) to work for a certain number of years, usually between four and seven, in return for his or her passage to the colonies and upkeep during the time of servitude. Such servants could be sold to another master, and colonies passed laws regulating the master-servant relationship, including the provision of "freedom dues," clothes, and other goods received at the end of a person's term of servitude. In many cases, this system proved unsatisfactory, as indentured servants were bound to their masters for only a limited number of years, and many ran away, never to be recovered, before their terms had expired.

Africans, however, were easier to deal with. They could be purchased outright, their skin color made them distinctive, and their heathen background made it easier to subject them to harsh treatment. Finally, there appeared to be a never-ending supply that would provide labor for all who needed it.

The Spanish began importing African slaves into America in 1517, and by 1540, some ten thousand were arriving in the West Indies every year.

But it was the Dutch, French, and ultimately the English who dominated the slave trade in the seventeenth century. In 1621, the Dutch States General chartered the Dutch West India Company and gave it a monopoly of African and West Indian trade. The Dutch challenged the Portuguese for control of the West African slave trade in mid-century, but frequent wars with both France and England weakened them after 1675. The French began organizing a slave trade in the 1630s with the founding of the French Company of the West Indies, but it was never economically successful. By the end of the seventeenth century, the French were just holding on to a small share of the African slave trade.

At the dawn of the colonial era, slavery as such did not exist in England. Medieval serfs were bound in certain ways to their feudal lords, but they still enjoyed some legal rights. In the sixteenth century, England began to place stricter controls on vagrants, beggars, and others who seemed to have no constructive role in society. These controls included branding and servitude for a period of years to the person who had turned the misfit in. Strict punishment awaited those who attempted to escape.

By the beginning of the seventeenth century, the concept of slavery was understood in England. A slave's freedom was nonexistent, and a slave was a slave in perpetuity rather than for a limited number of years. To some English thinkers, this equated to a loss of humanity, such as one might think of a captive taken in battle. An important factor here is that captives were strangers, people from another place, and they were often infidels. As it developed in the early colonial years, blacks from Africa fit the definition of a slave perfectly.

England first began carrying slaves from Africa to Spanish America in 1562, but the trade was not profitable until 1618 when King James I chartered the Company of Adventurers of London to engage in African slave trade. The Adventurers were not successful, however, and the Dutch brought most of the earliest slaves to the English settlements in North America. In 1672, Charles II chartered the Royal African Company and gave it a monopoly of England's slave trade. The company worked hard to drive the Dutch and French out of Africa and to suppress independent English slave traders. Ultimately, it too was unsuccessful and lost its charter in 1698. With other companies free to involve themselves in the slave trade, the slave population in the English colonies rose significantly after 1698.

The first slaves to come to the English colonies in North America arrived in Jamestown on a Dutch vessel in 1619. Few were concerned about the legal status of these Africans and, in the earliest censuses in Virginia, they were listed as servants, even to the point of having a limited term of servitude before achieving freedom. There were very few Africans in Virginia at this time, perhaps only 300 in 1650. Not until 1661 did the Virginia assembly give legal recognition to slavery, although after 1640, Africans were no longer indentured, and thus had no likelihood of achieving their freedom. For Virginia planters, it was an economic question, a way to solve the perpetual labor shortage problem.

In the middle colonies, and especially in New Netherland, slavery was instituted in the 1620s. The Dutch, who were active slave traders, used African slaves on their Hudson River valley plantations and continued to do so until 1664, when the English took control of the colony. On the whole, the Dutch treated their slaves humanely and occasionally gave them their freedom as a reward for long or loyal service. After 1664, slavery continued in New York as the English sought commercial advantages from their colonies, although the numbers remained small in the seventeenth century. In 1698, there were 2,170 slaves in New York, out of a total population of more than 18,000. Under English rule, slaves were more restricted in their freedom than they had been under the Dutch; one consequence of this was a serious slave uprising in 1712, which led to even more restrictive laws. The situation was different in Pennsylvania, where the Quaker influence dampened the enthusiasm for slavery. But slavery certainly existed in the colony, and even William Penn said that Negro slaves were preferable to white servants because of the control that could be exerted over them.

In New England, the first blacks came as servants rather than slaves. While slaves were present in New England during the entire seventeenth century, it was the slave trade and not the slaves themselves that suited the region's businessmen with their commercial orientation. Competition with European slave traders was difficult, however, and some New England traders went as far as Madagascar to find their cargoes of slaves. Late in the century, the slave-trading prospects of New England improved with the decline of the Dutch and the removal in 1698 of the English Royal African Company's monopoly. New England slave traders enjoyed their most profitable years in the early eighteenth century.

Although there were fewer slaves in New England than in other parts of colonial North America, Puritans justified the institution on religious grounds; slavery was a vehicle for Christianizing the heathen African, who would surely benefit in the long run from the grace of God. There were short-term benefits as well—Puritans recognized the sacrament of marriage for slaves and did not make them work on Sundays.

By 1700, the question of race became central to understanding the particular evil of slavery in America. That Africans were "black" had a profound influence on the English. From well before their first encounters with Africans, the English had placed negative connotations on the word black. Black meant dirty; it meant having "dark or deadly purposes"; it was the color of evil. White, on the other hand, was linked with purity, light, and cleanliness.

Black people confused scientists who could not understand why some American Indians living at the same equatorial latitudes as Africans were not also black, or why blacks brought to Europe failed to turn white after a while. To answer these questions, some turned to the Bible and concluded that either the "mark of Cain" or God's curse on Noah's son Ham and his descendants was the origin of black people, which made them God's cursed race. Although many refuted this notion, it persisted into the nineteenth century, when slavery proponents used it to justify slavery in the years before the Civil War.

Other factors that supposedly made black Africans suitable for slavery to the English in the seventeenth century were their heathenism and their perceived uncivilized behavior. Although the English were not much interested in converting Africans, despite the Puritans' claims to the contrary, they did claim that Africans' heathen beliefs were defects that distanced them from the English Christians. The perceived uncivilized nature of Africans, seen in the way they lived their lives, was also something that marked them as quite different from the English. Englishmen frequently likened Africans to beasts. This was seen in the way in which the slave trade was managed. Potential slaves were herded together, examined, and bought and sold, just like livestock.

INTERPRETIVE ESSAY
Julia A. Woods

Slavery was introduced into the English colonies of North America almost by accident in 1619 when a group of Africans arrived in Virginia, which was then a struggling English colony. These Africans are mysterious figures. We only know of them because John Rolfe, a leader of the Jamestown colony, wrote to a treasurer of the Virginia Company; and in that letter he noted casually that a Dutch man-of-war had arrived five months before at nearby Point Comfort, in the Chesapeake Bay, and the settlers had traded provisions for "20. and odd Negroes" [meaning some number greater than twenty]. It is not known whether the Africans came to Virginia directly from Africa or after a period of residence in the Dutch sugar islands in the Caribbean, nor is it known what happened to them after their arrival in Virginia. Their status as slaves was unclear, since the institution of slavery was not clearly defined by their English masters, who were more familiar with the practice of indentured servitude. (Much of the labor in the colony at that time was performed by English indentured servants, people who exchanged a period of service, usually five or so years, for the price of their passage from England to the New World. The person to whom labor was owed could trade or sell the labor contract like any other valuable commodity, so indentured servants could be "sold" during their period of service.) The twenty or so Africans in the Jamestown colony were the first arrivals in a huge migration of workers brought to the Virginia colony to work in the enormously profitable tobacco-growing business. The colonists at the time did not seem to be aware of the importance of that first transaction in 1619, which would ultimately have a profound effect on the future of Virginia and the rest of North America.

Slavery in Virginia did not start out as an important part of the colony's society. The institution changed as the need for laborers to work the tobacco fields became more acute and as fewer English people were willing to undertake the risks inherent in settling in Virginia. As the numbers of Africans and people of African descent in Virginia increased, the leadership of the colony began to regard them as a potential source of trouble and took steps to see to it that legal and social institutions existed to keep them subordinate. In time, slaves found that their status had become permanent and absolute, encompassing every aspect of their lives; in the end slavery would only be ended by a bloody civil war.

We can only guess what had happened to them before their arrival in Virginia, but try to imagine these things happening to you: You are kidnapped by strangers who force you to walk many miles from your home to a coastline you have never seen before. You may be sick, since the diseases here on the coast are new to you and you have no resistance to them. You are held here for a while, then put on an enormous ship, the likes of which you have never seen before. On the ship are men who look so strange to you they scarcely seem human. You are taken across an unbelievably vast body of water, tossed about in the tiny space allotted to you below the deck. The smell is horrible, a combination of unwashed bodies, feces, blood, vomit, and urine. You may know some of your fellow captives, or at least speak the same language, or they may all be foreign and speak some assortment of languages unrecognizable to you. Some of your fellow captives may have tried to escape by flinging themselves into the water, even though they know they will drown in that enormous sea. The slavers may order a blacksmith to pull out all the teeth of some especially stubborn slaves who fought back by biting. Many of your fellow captives will have died during this voyage. When you at last arrive at land, it is unlike any other place you have ever been: either an island covered with mile after mile of sugar cane, worked by people who look like your fellow captives at the command of people who look like the slavers, or a densely wooded, swampy-looking shore where, you soon learn, you are going to help your English "masters" become rich by working long hours to grow a plant called tobacco.

The English were trying to establish a colony in Virginia for a very basic reason: they wanted to improve their own situation in this life and in the next one. European powers had been sending ships and men to remote parts of the world in order to trade, bringing back exotic goods that could be sold at high profit. Ships returning with spices from India made their investors rich. Spanish explorers had made themselves and their country rich, bringing home gold and silver from Mexico and South America. The English sought to benefit similarly from colonies in North America. Both the Spanish and the English were also motivated by the desire to spread their religion, which would bring God's favor to themselves and their nation. Spanish friars worked hard to convert the native population of Mexico and South America, and the English similarly sought to expand their own Protestant religion in North America. It did not seem at all odd to them that their financial and religious interests were so closely related; instead, they assumed that God was on their side and would reward their efforts on behalf of the one true faith.

Most of the slaves brought to the English colonies in North America were from the coast and adjacent interior of western and west central Africa, brought by English traders either directly from Africa or after some time in the West Indies. English traders usually bought slaves in coastal trade centers along the West African coast, between the present-day countries of Senegal and Angola. This region was very diverse and difficult to describe in general: it included both densely forested areas and grasslands and supported several hundred different ethnic groups, some as culturally and linguistically different from each other as they were from Europeans. Some raised cattle and others were farmers. Some people lived in relative isolation while others had ties, by friendship, political alliance, or trade throughout the continent and beyond.

The smallest and most basic social unit in African societies was usually the household. This group would include parents, children, grandparents, and other relatives. The household also included any slaves, who may have, by long association with the family, been treated well and been recognized members of the household, though never quite the same as family. A person could be enslaved by violent means, either kidnapped or captured in warfare, and then was usually transported far from home to prevent future escape. One could also be enslaved by a judicial or religious proceeding, as punishment for a crime. More rarely, a person might enslave himself voluntarily because he could no longer afford to take care of himself, thus choosing dependence over starvation.

Slave trading in Africa has a long history. Extensive trade networks crisscrossed the continent. Beginning around C.E. 700 and continuing into the twentieth century slaves were traded north, across the Sahara. There were also slave trade routes east toward the Indian Ocean. Long-distance traders traveled from one trading center to another, dealing with agents who had their own local networks. Slaves were only part of a huge trade: ivory, copper, and hides from central Africa; metalware, figs, and dates from North Africa; palm cloth and salt from the coast. Europeans bought these goods and many more, including gold from the Gold Coast, but mostly they were interested in slaves.

When European traders appeared on the West African coast in the sixteenth century the scale of the slave trade increased dramatically. They traded cloth, metalware, horses, brandy, and rum for slaves. Though the statistics have been disputed, the most reliable indicate that between the sixteenth and nineteenth centuries, as many as fifteen million people were exported from Africa's Atlantic coast and more than nine million arrived in the New World, with some 1.5 million dying during the sea passage in between. This involuntary migration of people, known to historians as the Black Diaspora, scattered an astonishingly large number of people throughout the world. Though the number of slaves taken to the English colonies in North America was relatively low, around 5 percent of the total, this trade represented a substantial proportion of the English slave trade from around 1650 to 1800. (As it happens, the twenty or so slaves taken to Virginia in 1619 were not the first Africans to set foot in North America, as some had traveled with the Spanish *conquistadores* in their travels in Mexico and Florida.) While the English entered the slave trade after the Spanish and Portuguese, they were quick to see the potential profits in the trade. Later, American merchants based in New England took up the trade.

From the beginning, Englishmen were fascinated by West Africans. They had no firsthand knowledge of West Africa before 1530, when the first Englishmen went to Africa and returned to publish a detailed account of the journey. The descriptions of black-skinned people and their strange ways were of great interest to English readers. The differences between Africans and Europeans are important because they helped make it possible for Europeans to tolerate (and profit from) slavery. Historians have debated whether racism existed first, before slavery, or whether slavery, in all its dehumanizing cruelty, made the enslaver racist as a response. This debate is important to those seeking to understand the origins and meaning of present-day racism. Englishmen had long associated the word "black" with negative ideas, using the term to describe things they regarded with dread. Englishmen did not like the fact that West Africans were not Christian and not interested in converting. Also, English observers found West African culture shocking and strange; they often saw cultural differences as signs of immorality and inferiority rather than as merely different. Some historians have focused on these cultural differences to explain racism, while other historians looked more closely at English attitudes toward gender. They pointed out that Englishmen began, unconsciously, to regard people and places they encountered during their explorations with the same attitude they regarded women: they spoke of "virgin land" and described both the land and the people using words strikingly similar to words that they used to describe women. And in English culture at that time, women were entirely subordinate to men, legally and socially. Thus, it is argued, it seemed completely natural that these strange lands and people would need to be controlled and dominated, just as women were. Whatever one may conclude about this debate, it serves as a useful example of how historians grapple with difficult issues, including the shadowy origins of modern problems and the elusive nature of human evil.

Ironically, Englishmen, before they began to profit from slavery, had regarded the practice with disdain. They saw the institution as the business of Portuguese and Spanish, people the English tended to regard with scorn. They were aware of the role of slavery in the past. For example, slavery had been an important institution in Greece and the Roman Empire, and slavery is also mentioned in the Bible. Unfree labor, in the form of serfdom, had existed in feudal England but serfs had some traditional rights, while slaves were simply property, with no rights whatsoever. In the European view, slaves were outsiders, non-Christians, and usually captives taken in wars, such as during the Crusades. It would simply not have occurred to an Englishman to enslave a fellow Englishman, and any person to be enslaved would have to appear to be very different from himself. From the perspective of an Englishman, the human world was arranged, metaphorically speaking, as a series of out-wardly expanding circles: at the center were the English people, who represented the ideal of humanity; the next circle would include non-English white Protestants, such as the Dutch, who only fell short of per-fection by not being English. The people become more alien and imperfect as the rings move outward, with successive circles including European Catholics, such as the Spanish and Portuguese, and then per-haps North African and Turkish Muslims (whom the English tended to lump together under the term "Moors"), then finally reaching such peo-ple as non-Christian, dark-skinned West Africans, whose cultures and religious practices were utterly alien to an Englishman in the year 1500.

Englishmen were familiar with the institution of slavery but were not necessarily morally opposed to the practice. Slavery became more im-portant to Europeans with the discovery that tremendous profits could be made from growing sugarcane, first in the Canary Islands and later in the Caribbean. Sugarcane is a very labor-intensive crop, requiring year-round backbreaking work to plant and harvest. The most practical (and profitable) way to grow sugarcane was to use workers who could be forced to the point of exhaustion and who had no right to quit their jobs. The high profit to be made in the west was of great interest to ambitious Europeans. The Spanish had found great mineral wealth. There was big money in sugar, and the goal of most European monarchs was to claim some of this wealth and keep it out of the hands of their enemies. One of the problems with doing so was finding workers to extract the wealth from the land. The local indigenous population (called Indians, perpetuating Columbus's confusion about the exact location of the Caribbean islands and nearby North America) tended to fare badly when put to work, dying in large numbers from European diseases in some areas. It was difficult to bring enough European workers to the New World, though the English tried. How, then, could they make the colonies profitable?

The Virginia colony was settled with the idea that profits could be made even as Englishmen spread the Protestant faith and kept out their rivals, the Catholic Spanish and French. The English practice was for the monarch to grant the right to explore, settle, and extract profits to a group of wealthy investors, who paid the expenses of colonizing an area. The Virginia Company, for example, hoped to recoup their investments and make a profit from the settlement in Virginia. When Rolfe wrote his letter to the treasurer of the Virginia Company regarding the twenty-some Africans, he was essentially reporting to his employers. While the Virginia Company expected eventually to settle families in the Virginia colonies, the first settlers were mostly young men of middle-class origin. They were not sure exactly how the colony could be made profitable, but every possibility was explored. The local Indians did not wear lots of gemstones or gold or silver ornaments, which indicated that there was not the sort of mineral wealth here that the Spanish had found in Mexico and the Andes. Still, the possibilities seemed endless in this vast land.

The first settlers had trouble getting successfully settled at first. The colony at Roanoke, in present-day North Carolina, had failed entirely, and the Jamestown colony had problems of its own. There is some evidence of a terrible drought that made both water and food scarce and that the first settlers were not always the most hardworking or knowledgeable farmers. Nearby swamps, with the associated mosquitos, meant that mosquito-borne illnesses were rampant among the colonists. The difficulty of finding good water sources meant that water-borne illnesses were also common. Further, the local Indians, organized under the Powhatan confederacy, sensed correctly that the Englishmen intended to move into their territory. They attacked from time to time, often causing large numbers of casualties. For the first few years, colonists subsisted mostly on foodstuffs brought from England or traded from the Indians. The colony might have failed entirely if the English had not learned how to grow tobacco.

Growing tobacco became an enormously profitable undertaking in Virginia. The English market for tobacco brought high prices as more people became addicted to smoking. But growing tobacco required an enormous amount of work. First the seeds had to be planted and then the seedlings were thinned and transplanted into rows, with each plant set into a mound of dirt that had to be first loosened and piled up by someone wielding a hoe. The rows had to be kept weeded, so that the young plants were not choked out by weeds. As the plants got larger, the tobacco planter had to worry about the weather, as hail or heavy winds and rain could tear up the leaves, rendering them worthless because tobacco buyers would not buy leaves that were not whole. When harvest time arrived, the leaves had to be handled carefully to prevent tearing. The bottom leaves of each plant were picked first and the harvest continued for weeks as the slower-maturing upper leaves were picked, working their way up the plant until only a stem and the topmost leaves remained. As they were picked, the leaves were bundled and dried. The dried leaves were carefully packed into enormous barrels called hogsheads, which were rolled to the nearest river or navigable creek and onto boats for transport. There were very few roads suitable for transporting large loads in the Chesapeake region, so the ownership of land with water access was an important requirement for successful tobacco farming. Growing tobacco required year-round work, as the winter months, after the barrels had been shipped and before the next planting, were usually spent clearing new fields and repairing fences and tools. The backbreaking work of clearing fields, hoeing the rows, and picking the leaves required a substantial labor force. Most of the first settlers in Virginia were young men without families, so they did not have wives and children to help work in the fields. They needed workers who could be forced to put in long hours in the fields.

The system of indentured servitude had worked well for settling the colonies, and between 75 and 80 percent of the people who left England for the Chesapeake during the seventeenth century were indentured servants. Indentured servants were young, in their mid-teens to early twenties, and were drawn from the ranks of unemployed farm and factory workers. There were far more men than women among their ranks. Their motive for going to Virginia was typically simple: in Virginia, after they served their term of servitude, they could hope to buy land. In England, an island where land was limited, land ownership was the basis for membership in the ranks of the land-owning, voting English elite; a landowner in Virginia would have the same rights. Indentured servants presented some problems to those seeking workers for their plantations. The unhealthful climate in Virginia meant that many Englishmen became ill and died, especially the hardworking and underfed servants. After the term of service had expired, few were willing to sign on for another term, so the period of servitude was limited. The low ratio of women to men meant that there were few children being born to the servant class, so there were no native-born English children to employ on plantations. The system required a constant flow of servants from England, but as economic conditions improved there, fewer people were willing to sign on to such a risky endeavor as servitude in Virginia. Another group of people who represented a potential source of labor, the Indians in Virginia, was unwilling to work for the English and could easily resist any attempt to enslave them, either by armed resistance or by disappearing into the vast wilderness.

Africans as laborers had some important advantages over English servants. To some extent, they were resistant to the diseases that killed or incapacitated whites. White servants were prone to run away and some managed to reach other English colonies, where they disappeared into the white population. Africans' dark skin made that impossible. Running away into the backcountry was also difficult, since Indians were willing to return a runaway slave or servant for a bounty. Slavery proved to be more economically stable than servitude: a slave can be made to work for the rest of his life, not just for a period of years. Furthermore, a Virginia law passed in 1662 declared that the status of children follow that of their mothers, so female slaves could potentially generate more property for their owners, since their children would also be their owners' slaves. One can only imagine the feelings of a slave mother on the birth of a child, knowing as she did that her baby was also her owner's property, a slave for the rest of his or her life. A slave could hope to raise enough money to buy freedom for herself or her children, but that was extremely difficult. Later laws would make it more difficult for a slave to become free, either by self-purchase or through the kindness of a master, who might have freed a slave for faithful service.

As the English presence became more solidly established in the Virginia colony, the social order began to change. As the English population increased, the availability of land decreased. The best land, located along navigable waterways, had long been claimed. Movement into the backcountry was restricted by hostile Indians. One result was the appearance of a class of landless white men, unmarried because of the unfavorable ratio of men to women, and landless because there was none available. These men were angry that the wealthy tobacco growers along the coast made little effort on their behalf to open up the frontier. This anger led to Bacon's Rebellion in 1676, a series of skirmishes between poor frontiersmen and wealthier coastal residents. The rebellion persuaded many tobacco planters that African slaves were a better source of labor than white indentured servants, who presented a potential source of trouble after their term of service was up. Slaves, they reasoned, were never freed and so could be controlled. Another conclusion that they reached was that relationships between slaves or free blacks and poor whites were potentially very threatening. What if the two groups allied themselves in armed rebellion against the authorities? The prospect was alarming. Slaves had already demonstrated that they were capable of resisting their masters in a wide array of strategies including violence, running away for a few days, breaking tools, feigning illness, sabotaging crops, or other means.

Changes in the laws regarding slavery tightened the restrictions on slaves and clarified the differences in status between slaves and servants. The law tended to follow behind social practices: the first law making it clear that some "servants" were bound for life was passed in 1660, even though slaves had existed in the colony for some time. Another law, passed in 1667, made it clear that a slave could not be made free by converting to Christianity; this law meant that, for the first time, the essential difference between slave and master was race, not religion, since one Christian could now legally own another. The harsh treatment of slaves is apparent in another law, passed in 1669, that declared that should a master kill a slave in the course of punishment for failure to obey orders, the master would not be charged with a crime, as the law presumes that no one would willfully destroy his property. Laws passed in the 1700s placed greater restrictions on slaves and free blacks, punishing whites who socialized with blacks and white women who bore children by black men and prohibiting marriage between blacks and whites. The result of these laws is that a master literally had the power of life and death over his slaves. Another result was an increasing sense of white solidarity, wherein poor whites who did not own slaves identified themselves more with the wealthier slave-owning class than with black slaves, with whom they were strongly discouraged from socializing.

Historians have considered how it was possible that slavery became so important so quickly in the English colonies. Some argue that slavery was simply an economically rational solution to a labor problem: African slaves filled a need for labor on the sugar plantations and in the tobacco fields that otherwise could not be met. They point out that the uncertain status of the first Africans in the New World indicates that racism was not an important motivation in the initial decision to use unfree African labor. Other historians disagree: while slavery solved an economic problem, it was also based on an awareness of ethnic differences between Europeans and Africans that hardened rapidly into racial hatred; the fact that slavery was a status reserved for people of West African ancestry supports this argument.

The events of the seventeenth century set the stage for the next two

hundred years, though no one at the time could have expected the re-
sults. Slavery became increasingly important to the agricultural economy
of the South and less so in the North, where industrialization meant that
agriculture was not as important, and immigration ensured that labor
was more readily available. During the Revolution, some of the colonists
feared that the British government was determined to reduce them to
the equivalent of slaves, and Thomas Jefferson, himself a slaveholder,
wrote that "all men are created equal" and that a government that threatened the rights that every man possessed was doomed to failure. How
can we reconcile these beliefs to the fact that so many revolutionaries
themselves owned slaves? Some historians argue that it was this fact that
helped make these men revolutionaries, that the daily presence of slaves
and their powerlessness in the face of the utter control of slaveowners
served as an inescapable negative example. A slaveowner did not think
that he, personally, could be enslaved, but he would be the one who
determined that no man, no government, would ever have that degree
of power over him. And he would be prepared to risk a revolution to
prevent such a thing from happening.

There were, of course, other reasons for the Revolution besides some
slaveholders' anxiety about being reduced to helplessness. The Enlightenment, an intellectual current in European thought that, among other
things, asserted that all institutions should be evaluated on the basis of
their reasonableness, not merely respected as part of tradition. Every
human being, Enlightenment philosophers insisted, had a right to be
treated justly by a reasonable and humane government. American revolutionaries, unhappy with their treatment at the hands of the British
colonial authorities, found those ideas tremendously appealing. And
they were not oblivious to the irony of slave ownership in their midst.
They repealed laws making it difficult or expensive for a master to free
his slaves. Thomas Jefferson himself agonized about the cruelties of slavery and devised schemes to gradually end the institution in Virginia, yet
he personally freed only a handful of slaves, too deeply in debt to risk
the financial setback of the loss of his slaves. George Washington, himself
a rich man, freed his slaves in his will, as did a number of lesser-known
revolutionaries. Some, like Washington, were motivated by the obvious
contradiction between revolutionary principles and slave ownership and
others were also inspired by a deep Christian faith and the desire to do
right by their human property. Slaves themselves took action: many fled
to the British lines during the war in response to promises of freedom if
they deserted their masters. Many observers soon after the Revolution

believed that slavery was a doomed institution, that a long-term decline in tobacco production made slavery unprofitable.

Slaveowners had a more practical reason to regard slavery with dismay: the slaves on the island of San Domingue, a French sugar island, rebelled, defeated the French army, and created their own nation, the Republic of Haiti. No sensible slaveowner could regard his own slaves the same way after the news of that revolution. The news from San Domingue/Haiti caused some slaveholders to consider freeing their human property and others to seek to tighten control over their potentially rebellious slaves. What they could not anticipate was the invention of the cotton gin. The gin, which removed the seeds from the fuzz in cotton bolls, made it profitable to grow a variety of cotton plants that thrived throughout the South. Cotton is a labor-intensive crop and, in the days before mechanized farming, was most profitable when grown with the use of slave labor.

In the end, those who sought to control slaves more closely won. Slaveholders would continue to guard their rights with particular care, with the thought that weakness in the institution of slavery could lead to the situation that resulted in the Haitian revolution. Throughout the nineteenth century, southern politicians would seek to ensure that the institution would be allowed to expand westward with the growth of the nation and that laws would ensure that runaway slaves would be returned as swiftly as possible. They believed that the right to move into western territories with their slaves was essential to preventing the high ratio of black to white population that existed in Haiti before the revolution, by diffusing the slave population westward. Northern politicians became less sympathetic to these southern demands; slavery in the north had been ended and they saw the west as a land of opportunity for small farmers, not a place set aside for plantations worked by slaves. These differing views of the west, and by extension, of the American dream itself, were an essential source of regional conflict, a struggle that would eventually be settled by a bloody Civil War.

SELECTED BIBLIOGRAPHY

Berlin, Ira. *Many Thousands Gone: The First Two Centuries of Slavery in North America*. Cambridge, MA: Belknap, 1998. This book focuses on slavery from the perspective of the slaves and what they did every day, in the Chesapeake, South Carolina, and the Mississippi Delta.

Boles, John B. *Black Southerners, 1619–1869*. Lexington: University Press of Kentucky, 1984. As the title suggests, this book looks at African Americans in the cultural context of the Old South.

Brown, Kathleen M. *Good Wives, Nasty Wenches, and Anxious Patriarchs: Gender, Race and Power in Colonial Virginia*. Chapel Hill: University of North Carolina Press, 1996. Brown uses gender analysis in her approach to slavery and Virginia society. From this perspective, issues of race, gender, and religion take on whole new meanings.

Davis, David Brion. *The Problem of Slavery in the Golden Age of Revolution, 1770–1823*. Ithaca, NY: Cornell University Press, 1975. Davis addresses the conflicts between the rhetoric of the revolution and the ownership of slaves.

Degler, Carl N. *Neither Black nor White: Slavery and Race Relations in Brazil and the United States*. New York: Macmillan, 1971. The comparative approach adopted in this book provides an unusually insightful view of the subject of slavery.

Du Bois, W.E.B. *The Souls of Black Folk*. 1903. Reprint ed. New York: Penguin, 1996. Written by one of the most influential African-American leaders in the first half of the twentieth century, this book is part sociological and historical analysis and part manifesto. It is also prophetic: "The problem of the twentieth century is the problem of the color line."

Elkins, Stanley. *Slavery: A Problem in American Institutional and Intellectual Life*. Chicago: University of Chicago Press, 1959. Elkins created a storm of criticism when he depicted slavery as such a total system of oppression that slaves were reduced to childlike "sambos." His use of an analogy to World War II concentration camps was especially controversial.

Fogel, Robert, and Stanley Engerman. *Time on the Cross: The Economics of American Negro Slavery*. 1974. New ed. New York: W. W. Norton. 1995. This book is controversial both for the conclusion—that slavery was not as oppressive as others had depicted it—and for its approach, a purely numeric economic analysis based on slaveholders' records.

Fox-Genovese, Elizabeth. *Within the Plantation Household: Black and White Women of the Old South*. Chapel Hill: University of North Carolina Press, 1988. This book considers relationships between white and black women, concluding that the shared ties of womanhood were not enough to transcend the institution of slavery.

Franklin, John Hope. *From Slavery to Freedom: A History of African Americans*, 1947. 7th ed. New York: Knopf, 1994. This book is an authoritative and comprehensive history of African Americans from African civilizations up to the present.

Genovese, Eugene. *Roll, Jordan, Roll: The World the Slaves Made*. New York: Pantheon, 1974. This landmark book places greater emphasis on slave autonomy and culture, while not neglecting the essential oppressiveness of the institution itself.

Gutman, Herbert G. *The Black Family in Slavery and Freedom, 1750–1925*. New York: Pantheon, 1976. This well-researched book is a good choice for a reader interested in a longer view of the subject.

Hine, Darlene Clark, and Kathleen Thompson. *A Shining Thread of Hope: The History of Black Women in America*. New York: Broadway Books, 1990. A narrative survey covering four centuries of history, including individual stories of black women's struggles and accomplishments. It is well written and lively, a fascinating read.

Isaac, Rhys. *The Transformation of Virginia: 1740–1790*. New York: W. W. Norton, 1988. A fascinating and well-written book, useful for anyone interested in understanding colonial and Revolutionary-era Virginia.

Jordan, Winthrop. *White Over Black: American Attitudes Toward the Negro, 1550–1812*. New ed. New York: W. W. Norton, 1995. Originally published in 1969, this book explores the cultural and psychological origins of slavery and racism. Jordan's conclusions have been debated and criticized, yet his ideas remain compelling.

Kolchin, Peter. *American Slavery: 1619–1877*. New York: Hill and Wang, 1993. This clear and succinct book covers not only slavery in the United States but also in the Caribbean and Brazil, providing a description of how slavery developed and evolved.

Morgan, Edmund S. *American Slavery American Freedom: The Ordeal of Colonial Virginia*. New ed. New York: W. W. Norton, 1995. This book presents a good, brief coverage of slavery in the colonial era. It also offers a clear explanation of the connections between slaveholding and revolutionary ideology.

Parish, Peter J. *Slavery: History and Historians*. New York: Harper and Row, 1989. Parish presents a useful summary of the debates among historians about slavery.

Smith, Patricia. *Africans in America: America's Journey Through Slavery*. New York: Harcourt Brace, 1998. This book is the accompanying volume to the PBS television series and covers slavery from Africa, to the Atlantic crossing, and throughout the Caribbean and America up to emancipation.

Wood, Betty. *The Origins of American Slavery*. New York: Hill and Wang, 1997. This book provides a helpful and succinct presentation of its subject, covering not only Virginia but also Africa and the Caribbean.

Wood, Peter. *Black Majority: Negroes in Colonial South Carolina from 1670 through the Stono Rebellion*. New York: Knopf, 1974. This book offers an excellent survey of slavery in South Carolina in the colonial period, including the Stono Rebellion, one of the most fascinating episodes.

Wright, Donald R. *African Americans in the Colonial Era: From African Origins Through the American Revolution*. Arlington Heights, IL: Harlan Davidson, 1990. This book contains a useful and brief summary of colonial slavery, with interesting background information about slavery in Africa and the Caribbean.

This illustration of New Amsterdam in the 1660s suggests its small size and isolated location. (Reproduced from the Collections of the Library of Congress.)

7

The Surrender of New Amsterdam, 1664

INTRODUCTION

The Dutch explorer Henry Hudson first sailed up what is now known as the Hudson River in 1609, but his third voyage, in 1610, was particularly important because it proved to the Dutch government that the North (Hudson) River was a good place for settlement and trade, and that there was no water route extending from the river to the "western sea," where China and its fabulous treasures were supposed to be.

One of the first detailed geographical descriptions of the Dutch area of settlement was Johannes de Loet's *New World, or a Description of West-India*, published in 1625. De Loet was involved in Dutch business ventures in America, and his book appeared after the States General (the Dutch legislature) had chartered the Dutch West India Company in 1621. The company, which remained in control of New Netherland until 1664, enjoyed a trade monopoly among the Netherlands, the west coast of Africa, and all of America and could ally itself with native tribes and administer colonial government. In its earliest years, the Dutch West India Company was more interested in maintaining Brazil as a colony. In the early 1650s, the Dutch battled the Portuguese for control of Brazil and lost in 1654.

Despite its interest in Brazil, the Dutch West India Company began sending settlers to New Netherland in 1624, and the following year, appointed Willem Verhulst director general. Verhulst, however, took advantage of the distance between New Netherland and company headquarters to abuse his powers. A local advisory council he had established objected to his behavior and banished him from the colony. The council replaced Verhulst with Peter Minuit, a surveyor who had arrived in New Netherland with Verhulst.

The governmental and commercial center of the colony was New Amsterdam, located on the site of present-day New York City. New Amsterdam, like the rest of the colony, remained small during the early years of settlement. By 1643, its population was still fewer than 500 permanent residents, although there was considerable ethnic and religious diversity. The port facilities were busy but many who worked there were transients. In the late 1620s, Minuit tried to attract more colonists by initiating brick manufacturing and timber-cutting enterprises and by ordering the building of a ship larger than any then in the Dutch fleet. The ship, which probably weighed 800 tons, was finished in 1630 and christened the *New Netherland*. The ship became a part of the West India Company's transoceanic fleet, but the company directors never forgot how expensive the ship was to build, and the experiment contributed to Minuit's recall in 1631. Not long afterward, the Swedish government employed Minuit to lead New Sweden, its colonization venture in North America.

When the New Netherland colony did not become self-sufficient, as had been expected, the company introduced new initiatives to encourage greater immigration and economic activity. In 1629, company officials implemented the patroonship plan. Under this plan, one could become a *patroon* (or, a patron) if over the course of three years, one brought fifty new settlers to New Netherland. In return, the company granted the patroon four leagues (about eighteen miles) of land along one side of the Hudson River or two leagues along each side of the river. Settlers could move inland from the river as far as it was practical or safe. Within this domain, the patroon exercised administrative and judicial authority, although a colonist could appeal to the company in matters regarding serious offenses. Patroons were permitted to trade with anyone up and down the coast of North America, by paying a 5 percent tax to the company for the concession. In addition, all trade within the colony or between the Dutch and other colonists was supposed to flow through New Amsterdam so that the director general could keep track of it for tax purposes, but this was virtually impossible to enforce.

Several prominent investors applied for patroonships, but only the van

Rensselaer family possessed the wealth to establish a functioning community. In 1630, Kiliaen van Rensselaer established the patroonship of Rensselaerswyck. Several others tried but failed to create successful patroonships and sold their land back to the company. Although van Rensselaer remained prominent in New Netherland affairs for many years, the patroonship plan did not result in significantly increasing either the population or prosperity of New Netherland.

Although New Netherland was not founded for religious reasons, the Dutch West India Company was concerned about the spiritual needs of its settlers. The company established a Reformed Church in the colony, basically Presbyterian in nature. Congregations had a good deal of control over their own affairs, although they were nominally under the supervision of a body called the *classis*, which consisted of all the ministers in a particular district. The classis could install and remove ministers from their churches. Above the classis was the *synod*, a group of church leaders, which had broad supervisory authority. The first minister sent to the colony was Jonas Jansen Michielase, whose name was Latinized to Jonas Johannes Michaelius. He arrived in April 1628 and organized a church in Manhattan, the settlement near the port.

In addition, the patroonship arrangement also required patroons to provide a religious opportunity for the settlers within the domain, and van Rensselaer eventually called a minister to his patroonship. Johannes Megapolensis arrived in 1642 under a six-year contract. Megapolensis enjoyed the full confidence of van Rensselaer, who often consulted him on important administrative issues. In 1643, Megapolensis was one of the first Christian ministers to go out and preach to the Indians. After leaving Rensselaerswyck in 1649, Megapolensis was persuaded to preach in New Amsterdam and stayed there until his death in 1669.

After the controversy about the *New Netherland*, the Dutch West India Company replaced Minuit with Bastiaen Jansen Krol, who served only a year. The next director general was Wouter Van Twiller. The fourth director general of New Netherland was not a notable colonial administrator but his physical presence was remarkable, if the description of fictional chronicler Diedrich Knickerbocker is to be believed:

> He was exactly five feet six inches in height and six feet five inches in circumference. His head was a perfect sphere, and of such stupendous dimensions that Dame Nature, with all her sex's ingenuity, would have been puzzled to construct a neck capable of supporting it; whereupon she wisely declined

the attempt and settled it firmly on the top of his backbone,
just between the shoulders. . . . His legs were short, but strictly
in proportion to the weight they had to sustain, so that when
erect he had not a little the appearance of a beer barrel on
skids. (Quoted in Irving, p. 141)

Van Twiller's service in New Netherland lasted five years, all the while
plagued by his alcoholism and ineffectiveness. In 1638, he was replaced
by Willem Kieft, a hard-driving, ambitious director general whose eight
years in the colony were marked by worsening relations with the Indians
of the region. The economy and society of New Netherland were badly
damaged by a series of Indian wars between 1643 and 1647. At the end
of these wars, Peter Stuyvesant replaced Kieft as director general of New
Netherland. He was the last Dutch director general of the colony, honest
and capable but authoritarian to the point of being tyrannical.

As director general, Stuyvesant was interested in defending New
Netherland against its English and Swedish neighbors, in reining in the
independent patroons, like van Rensselaer, and in suppressing illegal
trading with the Indians, who were acquiring guns in that way. In 1650,
to pay for his policies, Stuyvesant convened representatives of the people, known as the Nine Men, to secure their assent to levy taxes. The
Nine Men came to represent a kind of political opposition to the director
general, expressing their displeasure over various issues and requesting
mediation in the Netherlands States General.

Stuyvesant opposed this challenge to his authority and tried to suppress the Nine Men, but they petitioned the States General, which, since
it was involved with Brazilian matters at the time, did nothing about the
dispute. Ultimately, Stuyvesant relented somewhat, gave "village
rights," including the right to establish local courts, to twelve settlements
and, in 1653, allowed New Amsterdam, the largest settlement, a limited
municipal government.

Stuyvesant's most important military action was the capture of Swedish settlements on the Delaware River in 1655. New Sweden was
founded in 1638 with some help from Dutch merchants, who could en-
vision a profitable trade relationship with the traditional friendly
Swedes. The Swedish South Company, responsible for the settling of
New Sweden, sent Peter Minuit to direct the new colony. Early Dutch-
Swedish relations were good; each colony controlled a bank of the Delaware River. Conflict arose, however, over Indian trade, disputed
purchases of Indian lands, and the aggressiveness of Stuyvesant's ad-

ministration. In 1651, he ordered the construction of a new fort on the South River very near Fort Christina of the Swedes. Relations worsened, and in 1654, New Sweden received a large number of reinforcements from Sweden, but further efforts to strengthen the colony's defenses were too late.

The Dutch West India Company ordered Stuyvesant to drive the Swedes out of their territory, and in August 1655, Stuyvesant organized the largest military force seen in any of the colonies along the Atlantic Coast. The Dutch forces sailed to the Delaware River in early September and forced the surrender of Fort Casimir on September 11. Ironically, the Dutch had built Fort Casimir in 1651, but the Swedes had captured it a year later. On September 24, Fort Christina capitulated, effectively ending the conflict and the Swedish presence in North America.

Conflict between the Dutch and the English over New Netherland dated back to 1621. The Dutch claimed the territory by virtue of prior discovery and occupation, while the English pointed to the proclamation of King James I in 1606 that granted the Virginia Company the right to colonize anywhere between 34 and 45 degrees north latitude, an area that easily encompassed New Netherland. English pressure mounted as the New England colonies grew much more rapidly than did New Netherland, and boundary disputes were frequent. Eventually, New Netherland was outmatched by the English presence, and directors general in the 1650s and 1660s permitted English settlements like New Haven to be established on territory the Dutch had originally claimed. A similar conflict regarding English settlement occurred on Long Island, although Stuyvesant did not object to independent English settlers coming to New Netherland.

In 1650, Stuyvesant and the English negotiated a treaty establishing a boundary running through both Long Island and present-day Connecticut. Although not ratified by the Dutch government until 1656 and never ratified by the English, the agreement worked to keep the peace for several years. After the restoration of King Charles II in 1660, however, the English government sought to streamline their North American colonial administration. Removing the Dutch from New Netherland would give the English control of the entire coastline, now that the Dutch themselves had eliminated New Sweden.

In 1662, Connecticut was given a new charter that extended its domain well into parts of New Netherland, ignoring the 1650 treaty. In the following year, Charles II, ignoring totally the existence of New Netherland, granted the land from the Connecticut River to the Delaware River to his younger brother James, then Duke of York. James organized a military force under the command of Colonel Richard Nicolls to go to New Netherland and secure his land. In late August 1664, Nicolls's forces landed in the harbor at New Amsterdam and demanded that Stuyvesant surrender the city, a move with which many Dutch people, aware of the futility of a fight, agreed. Stuyvesant held out for several days but finally yielded to the English on September 8, 1664.

New Netherland became the English colony of New York, except for a brief period in 1673, when during an Anglo-Dutch war, the Dutch navy captured New York. The city (if not the entire colony) remained under Dutch control for about fifteen months until the treaty ending the war returned New York to England.

INTERPRETIVE ESSAY
Thomas A. Mackey

While walking through the concrete, steel, and glass canyons of lower Manhattan today, it is difficult to believe that one walks in the footsteps of the original Dutch settlers of New Netherland where a wall separated the wilds of Manhattan from the Dutch city of New Amsterdam. Although Dutch heritage is difficult to find in lower Manhattan, a few Dutch place names survive such as Wall Street and Bowling Green. In other places in greater New York and up the Hudson River the Dutch presence can be heard in names such as "Breukelyn" (Brooklyn) and Haerlem. An Indian trail ran the length of Manhattan Island, ending at the Dutch settlement. In the late 1650s, the Dutch widened the path into their settlement. These improvements led the Dutch to refer to the path by the descriptive name "Breede Wegh," anglicized to "Broad Way." But these street and place names are the last vestiges of the Dutch presence in New York City. This essay examines the origins and development of the Dutch settlement of New Amsterdam and how the Dutch lost their North American colony to the English in September 1664. With the takeover of New Netherland, the English secured their hold on the eastern shores of North America and no longer feared any European threat from *within* their claims to coastal North America. Only the French in Canada loomed as a threat to the English holdings that stretched from Nova Scotia southward through the Chesapeake Bay.

In September 1609, Henry Hudson, an Englishman in the employ of the Dutch East India Company, reached the North American mainland north of Virginia. He guided his ship, *Da Halve Maen* (*The Half Moon*), into a navigable river that emptied into the Atlantic Ocean. He passed what would be known as Manhattan Island on his right and continued as far north as the river was navigable (to approximately the area of Albany). Along the way Native Americans met his ship and traded tobacco, corn, and furs for trinkets, beads, and knives. That river bears this explorer's name, the Hudson River, and his company claimed the excellent port at the mouth of the river where the Dutch West India Company founded New Amsterdam in 1624. Yet Henry Hudson was not the first to "discover" the river. One hundred years before the founding of New Amsterdam, the Italian explorer Giovanni da Verrazano anchored at the narrow entrance to the river. Today, the elegant Verrazano Narrows Bridge connecting Staten Island and Brooklyn is named in his honor.

Henry Hudson had not set sail to find new peoples or to start new colonies; rather, in his quest for the riches of Asia, he searched for a northwest water passage through the land mass. In this goal he failed, but his later explorations took him farther north where his name adorns Canada's Hudson Bay and Hudson Strait. His explorations proved controversial. Upon returning to Europe, Hudson put the *Half Moon* into Dartmouth, England, for repairs and his mixed crew of Dutch and English spread the word about their discoveries. England's government viewed Hudson's actions as disloyal because he sailed for a potential competitor, the Dutch, and briefly imprisoned him. What bothered the English most was not Hudson's voyages, but rather his claim for the Dutch of the entire Hudson River area. In particular, the Plymouth and Virginia Companies of London claimed the entire coastline in their royal charters even though they possessed no practical means to enforce those claims. As a result, the Dutch, the Swedes, the French to the north, and the Spanish to the south ignored English declarations of ownership and carved out areas of the new world for themselves.

Like their British rivals, the Dutch employed a particular form of organization to undertake their exploration and colonization ventures— the joint-stock corporation. In the late sixteenth and early seventeenth centuries, Dutch economic energies and banking successes resulted in a prosperous Holland. Because of their economic success, many Dutch had money to invest in risky but potentially lucrative overseas voyages. In order to spread the risk of such voyages, the Dutch (like the British) developed joint-stock companies. By allowing a large number of people to invest in one company, more capital could be raised to fund voyages than any one investor might be able to finance, and, if the voyage failed, no one investor lost all of his investment. Because of these economic advantages, Dutch and English authorities regularly chartered joint-stock companies for exploration and colonization purposes.

By October 1614, the Dutch East India Company had lost interest in the New World and concentrated its trade efforts in the fur trade with Moscow. As a result, the Dutch States General chartered a new company, the New Netherland Company, to enter the North American fur trade. This company had a monopoly to make four voyages in the following three years, and the fur trade flourished. When the monopoly ended in 1617, the proprietors of the New Netherland Company sought to renew its charter but other investors lobbied the States General and prevented the awarding of another charter until June 3, 1621. On that date, a competing group of investors, the Dutch West India Company, received a charter and the exclusive privileges to control Dutch trade with New Netherland. Under this 1621 charter, the Dutch West India Company possessed the authority to maintain military forces, to negotiate trade and peace terms with the local peoples, and to administer its own affairs in the Americas and West Africa. As part of this charter, the Dutch States General required the company to "advance the peopling of those fruitful and unsettled parts."

In April 1624, the ship *Nieu Nederlandt* reached the Hudson River. Captained by Cornelius Jacobsen May, the *Nieu Nederlandt* carried thirty families whose goal was to establish a Dutch colony in New Netherland. These families came from southern Holland, were Protestants, spoke French, and were known as the Walloons. May sent eighteen of these families up the Hudson River to settle permanently at Fort Orange (near present-day Albany). He also dispatched settlers southward to Burlington Island in the Delaware River and others eastward to the Connecticut River valley. Only a few families remained on Noten (Governor's) Island and on Manhattan Island. May scattered these people because of Holland's disputed claims to the Hudson River area. May and the company directors sought to show that the Dutch had occupied their claimed territory.

In 1625, the company sent out six relief ships carrying provisions and hundreds of new Dutch colonists. Willem Verhulst was the commander of this expedition and, upon its arrival, he became the first director general of New Netherland. Verhulst had orders from the Nineteen Directors of the company to establish a permanent agricultural community in

New Netherlands. To centralize his control, Verhulst recalled to New Amsterdam the outlying Walloon settlements; after 1626, those trading outposts were staffed only seasonally. Verhulst also ordered that any other directors of the company who might be in the colony to serve as an advisory council to him; but, because few of the major investors ever visited the far-flung colony, the director general wielded almost unchecked power throughout the Dutch period.

Political power in the hands of one director general could become a problem and Verhulst was the first to abuse his powers. He lost key support among the settlers by berating the settlers for not spending enough time working on the company's lands and for his harsh punishments for minor crimes. When it came to light that Verhulst had altered the company's books to enrich himself, the council banished him from the colony. Succeeding Verhulst was Peter Minuit, who had come to New Netherland to help Verhulst survey the area.

One of the persistent questions of this early period is how and when did the Dutch "buy" Manhattan Island from the local Indians? The traditional account holds that Peter Minuit purchased the island for sixty florins worth of trade goods from the local Mahican tribe in 1626. Historians challenge this story, arguing that Willem Verhulst actually arranged the exchange of goods for the Dutch settlement on Manhattan Island and that Minuit bought Staten Island. What actually occurred remains unclear. Because Indians did not think in terms of "owning" land as Europeans did but rather understood land as something that supported all people, one wonders whether the Mahicans considered their exchange for Manhattan a final "sale" or saw the exchange as a "gift" for the right of the Dutch to settle. What is clear is that by the fall of 1627 New Netherland was taking shape, with its political and commercial center at New Amsterdam on Manhattan Island. In addition to thirty houses there, the colonists finished an unimpressive fort or blockhouse surrounded by a log and earthen palisades.

But all was not well. The Dutch West India Company, with its major investments in Africa and elsewhere in the Americas, expected the small colony to become self-sufficient quickly. Yet, the colony did not boom as investors hoped. Agricultural production failed to meet expectations, lumber proved expensive to harvest and ship, and the fur trade (the only true "cash crop" of the colony) slowed.

To address these problems, the Dutch West India Company loosened its hold over the colony and allowed more private initiative and investment. In 1629, the company implemented the patroonship plan, whereby a wealthy individual could acquire a large amount of land in return for recruiting colonists for New Netherland. Unfortunately for the Dutch, the patroonship plan did not prove successful. Few Dutch investors had the capital to establish patroonships, and few Dutch settlers were willing to work the large farms. The most successful of the patroonships, Kiliaen van Rensselaer's Rensselaerswyck, struggled during the 1630s, and most of the other patroons eventually sold their land back to the company. In the end, the patroonship plan failed to meet the key need of New Netherland—more colonists.

To meet this need the company revised its charter again in 1629 to allow less prominent people to receive land titles in New Netherland. Under these new terms people who settled in the colony could receive title to a certain amount of land. This also failed to generate adequate immigration so in 1639 the company expanded its offer by granting as much land as people could cultivate. To sweeten the deal even further, the company granted colonists the right to control their property in perpetuity. In return, the settlers had to pay a tax, a quitrent, of one-tenth of the value of their produce and their cattle herds to the company. In 1640, building on these incentives, the company offered two hundred acres of land to settlers who brought five immigrants to the colony and offered limited self-government to those who established towns or villages. One glitch to these plans was the Indian claims to the land that had to be cleared *before* the company recognized the settlers' land titles. This requirement led to widespread fraud and cheating by the Dutch settlers. Not surprisingly, this issue generated so much bad feeling between the Dutch and the Indians that in 1652, Director General Peter Stuyvesant forbade private land purchases from the Indians without the consent of the company.

When experiments with land offerings failed to attract large numbers of Dutch settlers, New Netherland opened its doors to almost anyone willing to settle. Eventually the colony grew, but not necessarily with Dutch immigrants and certainly not quickly. New Netherland numbered about 300 people in 1630 and five hundred in 1640; by 1664 when the English conquered New Amsterdam, the colony contained fewer than nine thousand settlers. At the same time the English colony of Virginia had a population of approximately forty thousand people and New England had fifty thousand. New Amsterdam attracted a wide diversity of people (Dutch, English, French) and religions (Protestants, Catholics, and even Jews), a tradition that has continued throughout New York City's rich history.

Dutch governance in New Netherland suffered from weak leadership. Director General Peter Minuit lasted until 1631 when the directors of the company recalled him after the controversy over the building of the *New Netherland*. After Minuit, Bastiaen Jansen Krol arrived but served only a year, and the alcoholic ex-company clerk Wouter Van Twiller followed him, in turn, in 1633. Van Twiller lasted five years only to be followed in 1638 by the ambitious, heavy-handed, and imprudent Willem Kieft. Because of his rash policies and bad relations with the Native Americans, intermittent fighting with the Indians resulted. These attacks, combined with his harshness as director, led to a general call from within the colony for Kieft's removal, which occurred in 1646. New Netherland's last director general was the combative, pious, military veteran Peter Stuyvesant who arrived in New Amsterdam in May 1647. Stuyvesant's tenure was not without controversy as he feuded with both his fellow Dutch settlers and his English neighbors, but he did bring stability and better leadership to the Dutch colony.

A principal area of simmering tension between the British and the Dutch lay to the northeast, in the Connecticut River valley. Both the English in New England and the Dutch from New Netherland sought to control the lucrative Indian fur trade along that river. Their rivalry demonstrated the weakness of the Dutch and the determination of the English to claim the hinterlands of New England. What made the Connecticut River valley so important to both groups was its geography—it flowed from deep in the heartland of New England. Indians used this natural highway to move their pelts of beaver and otter out of the countryside and down to the European trading posts. Dutch leaders and traders wanted control of the river so that the Connecticut River did not siphon trade away from the Hudson River; English leaders and traders hoped to cut into the Dutch trade by controlling the river.

In 1633, Director General Van Twiller sent Jacob van Curler and a company of soldiers to establish a Dutch presence on the Connecticut River. Van Curler and his men built a small fort and trading post a few miles up the river and named it the House of Good Hope. Soon Indians appeared and the Dutch started doing a healthy business trading cloth, mirrors, and knives for furs.

Dutch advances into Connecticut caused concern in both the Pilgrim settlement of Plymouth and in the Puritan settlements centered around Boston. Pilgrim Governor Edward Winslow had opened negotiations with the Indians of the area but had not established a presence in the region. Upon hearing of the Dutch trading post, the Pilgrims began to outfit an expedition to establish their own presence on the river. Puritan Governor John Winthrop did not openly support Winslow's more aggressive actions, but he did write a sharp letter to Van Twiller restating the English claim to the area and warning the Dutch not to build fortifications there. Van Twiller responded that the Dutch West India Company's claim to the Connecticut River valley predated any English claim and that the House of Good Hope was only a trading post.

While Van Twiller and Winthrop exchanged letters, the Pilgrims sent a ship up the Connecticut River and set up their own trading post not far from the House of Good Hope. Van Twiller sent troops there with orders to eliminate the English. The Dutch commander, however, decided not to attack the English and withdrew to the House of Good Hope. More and more of the Indians took their furs to the English settlement for trading. This Dutch failure of nerve encouraged the English to continue their expansion in Connecticut. The House of Good Hope became merely a Dutch outpost amid a growing English colony.

Because of Van Twiller's alcoholism, the company recalled him in 1637 and appointed the strong-willed Willem Kieft the new director general for the colony. By appointing Kieft, the company sought to bring effective leadership to the colony and to place it on a better financial footing. In addition, the company tried to attract more settlers by liberalizing its policies on fur trading. Individual settlers could now enter into the lucrative trade, and private shippers could now handle the transportation of the furs.

As director general, Kieft caused more difficulties for the colony than he solved. Although he possessed some understanding of Indian culture and customs, he also believed that the Indians posed a problem for the Dutch fur trade. Kieft feared that the Indians would shift their trading relationship away from the Dutch to the English. In 1639, he placed a tax, a *contributie*, on Indians living within New Netherland, and he required that this tax be paid in pelts. His goal was to regularize the relationship between the Dutch and the Indians; instead, his policy resulted in a bloody war between the two peoples. There were misunderstandings about tax collection procedures and rumors about Indian raids on Dutch farms that prompted Kieft to order troops to destroy an Indian village and issue a proclamation offering a bounty for dead Indians. With this defiant attitude, Kieft virtually guaranteed that the conflict between the Dutch and the Indians would be neither short nor bloodless.

In 1641, the level of hostility increased after the brutal murder of a

Dutch wheelwright, Claes Smits. Kieft prepared his troops for war, and in February 1643, the Battle of Pavonia resulted in the deaths of 180 Indians, including women and children. That bloody event led to reprisals from Indians up and down the Hudson River in 1643 and 1644 in which numerous Dutch and English settlers on outlying farms were killed. Among them were the noted dissenter from the Massachusetts Bay Colony, Anne Hutchinson and her children. Indian attacks so crippled the colony that the Dutch had to send food to New Amsterdam because so many Dutch farms had been abandoned.

After hearing numerous complaints about Kieft and the Indian war, the Nineteen Directors of the West India Company recalled the director general, instructed the remaining Dutch to sign a peace treaty with the Indians (which they did), and started a search for a new leader. Although they did not know it, their choice proved to be the colony's most colorful and important director general, Peter Stuyvesant.

On May 11, 1647, Stuyvesant arrived in New Amsterdam. The new director general cut quite a picture. A military man and an ardent Dutch nationalist, Stuyvesant had served in the Caribbean and in 1644 had led an assault on a Spanish fort on the island of St. Martin. During the battle, a cannon shot cost him his right leg. He learned to walk again using a wooden peg leg that he adorned with silver bands. A devout Calvinist, Stuyvesant expected obedience and was both energetic and autocratic. These qualities made him an impressive and influential leader.

Although Stuyvesant brought stability to the colony, his personality and actions could not ultimately preserve New Netherland. International developments out of his control and the failure of the Dutch to people their North American claim caused the loss of New Netherland. But for seventeen years, Stuyvesant presided over the colony and sought to stem the rising tide of English colonies and colonists.

Boundary disputes between the Dutch and the Indians continued throughout Stuyvesant's administration, resulting in the Esopus War. This conflict started in 1659 at the Dutch village of Esopus (now Kingston), about halfway between New Amsterdam and Beverwyck. Tensions had been mounting in the area because some of the Dutch residents traded brandy for furs. Drunk Indians harassed the Dutch, invaded farms, and murdered one Dutch resident. Stuyvesant traveled to the area and spoke with the Indian leaders. He believed he had achieved an agreement for the Indians to move farther inland and to stop harassing the settlers, but as soon as he left, the annoyances started again. On September 28, 1659, a local Dutch settler, Thomas Chambers, gave eight

Indians brandy in exchange for their help in husking corn. They proceeded to get roaring drunk and spent the evening making a great noise just outside the Dutch settlement. Seizing the opportunity, the Dutch attacked, killing two Indians and capturing one. In retaliation, other Indians swept through the surrounding countryside destroying crops, killing livestock, and burning Dutch barns and houses. Heavily outnumbered, the Dutch drew up a petition to Stuyvesant imploring that he return to Esopus immediately and save them. Eighteen of the settlers, eight soldiers, and their sergeant made their way to the river and sent the petition downstream but were surrounded and captured; only seven of the men managed to return safely. Unable to defeat the Dutch in their defensive blockhouse, the Indians took out their frustrations on their prisoners by torturing them and eventually burning them to death. Dutch reprisals continued well into the summer of 1660 before the director general and the Indian leaders signed a new peace agreement.

Equally troubling throughout Stuyvesant's years as governor were his European neighbors. On September 23, 1650, Stuyvesant appeared in Hartford, Connecticut, to meet with representatives of the United Colonies (a defensive arrangement of the English New England colonies) in an effort to settle the boundary dispute between New Netherland and New England. Their first clash concerned Stuyvesant's reference in his opening statement to Hartford, Connecticut, as part of "New Netherland." This description irritated the English representatives who asked him to stop using that label; he agreed, but only if the English stopped referring to Hartford and the Connecticut River valley as "New England." Reluctantly they agreed and the meeting got down to serious negotiations. The Hartford Treaty that emerged from this meeting skirted the issue of which side had permanent claims to the disputed areas, but it did clarify the division of territory, especially on Long Island, where the English had been allowed to settle for some twenty years. Under this treaty, the representatives drew a line of demarcation from western Oyster Bay on the north shore of Long Island south across to the Atlantic Ocean. Another boundary line was drawn on the mainland north from Greenwich Bay, near present-day Stamford; the Dutch agreed not to settle within six miles of this line. Stuyvesant agreed to the loss of two-thirds of Long Island and the Dutch claims around Hartford and much of the Connecticut River valley in order to protect Dutch holdings on the Hudson River. What the Hartford Treaty really accomplished was to describe and protect where the Dutch actually lived: Stuyvesant conceded no territory where the Dutch had permanent settlements. Although neither home government ratified the treaty promptly, New Englanders and New Netherlanders abided by its terms through the rest of the history of the Dutch colony.

In 1651 the economic rivalry between the British and the Dutch escalated when the British Parliament, in an effort to control its overseas trade, passed a Navigation Act requiring all of its foreign trade to be carried on in English ships with English crews. Directed at cutting into the Dutch trade, this 1651 Navigation Act led to a naval war between the two rivals. In North America, war panic emerged with the English convincing themselves that the Dutch were arming the Indians against them while the Dutch feared a full English assault. In the summer of 1653, New Netherland's last trading post in New England, the House of Good Hope, surrendered to the English. In June 1654, four English warships carrying troops and marines arrived in Boston with orders to invade New Netherland. But, just before the fleet was due to sail, a merchant ship arrived in Boston carrying news that the Anglo-Dutch War had ended. New Netherland had been saved—for now.

In 1660, the English civil war ended with the restoration of the British monarchy. Charles II returned to England and assumed his place as king. In early 1663, to reward his brother, James the Duke of York and Albany, for aiding him in regaining the throne, Charles II gave James control of the area in North America claimed by the Dutch. This gift took the form of a proprietary grant that ignored Dutch claims and Dutch settlements and left James to figure out how to take possession of it. James and his friends developed a plan for the military invasion of New Netherland. While the plan was costly, James hoped that control of the fur trade would more than cover their expenses of taking over the Dutch colony.

Charles II's gift and James's plan dovetailed with international events. Economic rivalry persisted, and an undeclared naval and colonial war already existed between the British and the Dutch. On March 12, 1664, James received his grant from Charles II, officially giving him control of the Hudson River valley area. This enabled James to put his plan for the capture of New Netherland into operation. In May, he sent Colonel Richard Nicolls with a small fleet and two thousand soldiers to North America.

Storms and bad sailing luck scattered the fleet. Nicolls hoped to be assembled near eastern Long Island by late June, but all of his ships did not arrive until late July. Stuyvesant heard reports about the possible takeover of New Netherland and wrote the company for advice. The directors erroneously assured Stuyvesant that the English expedition sought only to bring the Puritans under greater English control.

Nicolls moved his flagship, the *Guinea*, and his fleet along the south shore of Long Island, and on August 26 anchored in Graveshead Bay just south of the narrows between Long Island and Staten Island. At his disposal, Stuyvesant had about 150 soldiers, some of the local townspeople, and a dilapidated fort that could neither be adequately defended nor hold the town's 1,200 residents. Stuyvesant sent a messenger to Nicolls to inquire about the intentions of the British, and Nicolls demanded, quite simply, that Stuyvesant turn the town over to him. To emphasize his point, Nicolls moved his ships through the narrows and anchored them near Governor's Island. On September 2, 1664, Stuyvesant answered Nicolls's demand by declaring that the area had always been Dutch and would always remain Dutch. Nicolls brushed aside Stuyvesant's appeal to history and gave him forty-eight hours to surrender the city.

Between September 4 and September 6, Stuyvesant lost the support of burgomasters from the town. These prominent citizens were impressed with the generous terms offered by the English, whose spokesman, John Winthrop, Jr., the governor of Massachusetts Bay Colony, promised that immigration from the United Provinces of Holland and Dutch trade with the colony could continue. The frustrated Stuyvesant hesitated as the English moved their ships into positions that would allow them to bombard New Amsterdam from the river. At that, the director general hurried to the fort and prepared to fire on the English, but cooler heads intervened. One of the most respected of the burgomasters, Dominie Megapolensis and his son Samuel went to the fort, spoke briefly to Stuyvesant, and led him away before he ordered the cannons to fire.

Cornered and isolated, Stuyvesant now understood that his role had become one of carrying out the wishes of the people of New Amsterdam. He arranged a meeting of representatives of the English and the Dutch for the next day, September 6, at his own farm just outside the city, where they drew up a treaty surrendering the colony to the English. On September 8, 1664, Stuyvesant signed the document ending Dutch control of New Netherland, led his soldiers out of the fort, and marched them down to the Dutch ship, the *Gideon*. Once the Dutch had boarded their ship, Colonel Nicolls landed his forces and raised the Union Jack. New Amsterdam had become New York.

A few months after the fall of New Amsterdam, Great Britain and the

United Provinces of Holland formally went to war in what is known as the Second Anglo-Dutch War of 1665–1667. England's victory in this war legitimized James's takeover of New Netherland. But the struggle for dominance was not quite over, as the Dutch and the English fought yet another conflict, the Third Anglo-Dutch War of 1672–1674. On August 8, 1673, eight Dutch warships entered New York City's harbor and anchored. They found the city with the English governor gone and the fort undermanned. The Dutch demanded the surrender of the fort, and after a brief display of cannon fire, the English capitulated. The Dutch held New York for fifteen months. Their occupation ended with the signing of the Second Treaty of Westminster on February 19, 1674; a section of the treaty promised that each side would return to the other "all lands, islands, towns, ports, castles and fortresses" taken during the war. On November 10, 1674, the Dutch administrator boarded a ship and left New York; the last gasp of Dutch control had ended.

With Dutch claims extinguished, England controlled the coastline of North America from the Chesapeake northward. While the Swedes and the Dutch had established claims to areas within Great Britain's interest, they had failed to populate their colonies adequately. In the case of the Dutch in New Netherland, inconsistent leadership, half-hearted support from the West India Company, and occasionally severe Indian troubles all combined to prevent the Dutch from succeeding with their North American colony. While Peter Stuyvesant brought order and stability to New Netherland, English encroachment from New England and Long Island could not be held back. In the end, only Stuyvesant stood alone on the battlements of New Amsterdam's rickety fort ready to defend Holland's possessions.

In the short run the Dutch West India Company failed and the Dutch lost their toe-hold to an area of British North America; yet, their efforts in the long run were not in vain. From Henry Hudson to Peter Minuit's "purchase" of Manhattan Island to Peter Stuyvesant's last defense of the city, the Dutch formed a key part of the history of America's most important city.

SELECTED BIBLIOGRAPHY

Burrows, Edwin G., and Mike Wallace. *Gotham: A History of New York City to 1898*. New York: Oxford University Press, 1999. Surveys the history of New York City from the Indian era through the late nineteenth century.
Irving, Washington. *Knickerbocker's History of New York*. Introduction by Andrew

B. Myers. Tarrytown, NY: Sleepy Hollow Press, 1981. Washington Irving's delightful parody of the history of New York contains more sound history than the casual reader might imagine.

Kammen, Michael. *Colonial New York: A History.* New York: Charles Scribner's Sons, 1975. Provides important revisions to the story of early New York colonial history and continues to influence historians.

Kenney, Alice P. *Stubborn for Liberty: The Dutch in New York.* Syracuse, NY: Syracuse University Press, 1975. Covers the political history of Dutch New York as well as providing a social history of the colony.

Rink, Oliver A. *Holland on the Hudson: An Economic and Social History of Dutch New York.* Ithaca, NY: Cornell University Press, 1986. The most recent and important of the histories of Dutch New York building on and correcting Kammen's interpretation.

Ritchie, Robert C. *The Duke's Province: A Study of New York Politics and Society, 1664–1691.* Chapel Hill: University of North Carolina Press, 1977. Though focused on the period after the English takeover, the early chapters provide an interesting and useful synthesis of the historical literature of Dutch New York.

Smith, William, Jr. *The History of the Province of New-York.* Volume One: *From the First Discovery to the Year 1732.* Edited by Michael Kammen. Cambridge, MA: Harvard University Press, 1972. Reprint of one of the important early books on New York, reprinting some of the key Dutch and English documents while defending the English conquest of the colony.

Van Der Donck, Adriaen. *A Description of the New Netherlands.* Edited by Thomas F. O'Donnell. Syracuse, NY: Syracuse University Press, 1968. Originally published in 1656, this work describes and promotes the New Netherlands colony.

Van Der Zee, Henri, and Barbara Van Der Zee. *A Sweet and Alien Land: The Story of Dutch New York.* New York: Viking Press, 1978. A popular history of the Dutch in New York stressing the cultural and social conditions of the colony while providing some political history.

8

King Philip's War, 1675–1676

INTRODUCTION

When New England was first settled, many of the area's Indians had died in a smallpox epidemic in 1616. Not until after 1630 and the great increase in European migration to New England did tensions begin to rise between white settlers and Indians, and these became particularly acute with the settlement of Connecticut after 1630, which impinged on Pequot lands. This led to the bloody Pequot War of 1637.

In the forty years between the Pequot War and King Philip's War, Europeans and Indians lived in a state of continuing tension. Some Indians abetted colonial economic growth by working for colonists, selling meat and fish, and trading in wampum currency. Some were converted to Christianity, and these "praying Indians" often became military allies in conflicts between colonists and other Indians.

Despite some degree of economic cooperation and religious conversion, however, Indian-white conflict continued in New England after the Pequot War. Expansion into Connecticut and the creation of the colony of Providence Plantations (Rhode Island) served only to whet colonists' thirst for more land, and everyone realized that if more land were placed under colonial jurisdiction, more land would be available for individual settlers. Thus efforts to assume dominion over additional land, whether

Seventeenth-century Indian wars featured fighting at close quarters, as seen in this engraving from the nineteenth century. (Reproduced from the Collections of the Library of Congress.)

occupied by Indians or not, played an important role in colonist-Indian relations in the mid-seventeenth century. Intercolonial rivalry also exacerbated some of the moves to acquire more land.

In 1645, when the New Englanders denied the Narragansett Indians permission to attack the Mohegans, and they did anyway, the colonists raised a force and brought about the capitulation of the Narragansetts. In the 1650s, the whites again put down an Indian force and obtained land from Indians in Connecticut as part of the settlement.

New England's colonies grew rapidly during the period between 1650 and 1675. The population doubled to some fifty thousand and settlements spread into more backwater areas and encroached more and more on Indian lands. The Indians, bitter toward the English and unwilling to leave ancestral territory, became increasingly resentful. In the 1660s, the English forced the Wampanoag leader Metacom, whom they called King Philip, to recognize their sovereignty over all Indians. Many Indians came to the conclusion that armed resistance was the only way they could preserve their independence.

By the 1670s, English colonists particularly coveted the land of the large Narragansett tribe. It lay along the shore of what is now Rhode Island and southeastern Connecticut west from Narragansett Bay and included several islands in the bay. The English Crown had never granted a royal charter for this land to anyone, although some Englishmen, like Roger Williams, had moved there anyway. The Indians had tolerated this incursion, coming as it did fairly soon after the Pequot War. Moreover, Williams was known as an Indian ally in their struggles with the Massachusetts Bay and Connecticut colonies.

King Philip lived near the settlement of Bristol, in Rhode Island, at a place overlooking Narragansett Bay. In the early 1670s, militant Narragansett leaders approached him with an offer for the Wampanoags to join the Narragansetts in war against the land-hungry colonists, who were constantly trying to acquire more land in exchange for trinkets, liquor, or weapons. Indian attitudes grew more warlike, and Philip finally agreed that war was necessary. In June 1675, war broke out after an incident in which a farmer shot and wounded an Indian who had killed one of his oxen. Indians congregated in the area around Swansea, fighting began, and a number of settlers were killed. A force of 120, under Captain Thomas Savage, went to Philip's home, surprised him, and killed fifteen Indians. Although Philip himself managed to escape, Savage's force took his cattle and destroyed the rest of his property.

The Indian force under Philip then overran the colonial settlement of Mendan and almost took Brookfield, which was saved only by the timely arrival of additional colonial militia. At the same time, King Philip broadened his alliance; only the Mohegans, traditional enemies of the Narragansetts, refused to break a treaty made with settlers and join with Philip. It was a bad decision. The governor of Connecticut Colony, Edward Wilson, sent a force of colonial fighters to a fortified village of the Mohegans, and a major battle ensued. In what became known as the Great Swamp Fight, the village fell to the colonists and more than 300 Indians, including women and children, were killed. The outcome of the Great Swamp Fight made the Indians even more determined to resist colonial encroachment, and over the next several months, they attacked numerous white settlements throughout Massachusetts and Rhode Island, causing many casualties.

Philip next tried to lure the powerful Mohawk tribe into his alliance, but this effort failed and demoralized some of Philip's supporters. Nevertheless, the fighting continued with Philip's attack on Deerfield, a settlement in Massachusetts. At the same time, however, other Indians, weary of the warfare, were covertly seeking peace. They arranged for the capture of Philip's wife and child, who were shipped off to Bermuda as slaves, and Philip himself was killed by one of the dissenters.

Although the fighting continued for a few more months, King Philip's War was over by December 1676. The final count showed that 600 colonists (and many more Indians) had been killed, and thirteen colonial villages had been destroyed. But the colonists emerged from the war more unified, because of the cooperation utilized to subdue the Indians. New England Indian society, on the other hand, was weakened and fragmented, opening new lands for white settlement.

In the South, Jesuit and Franciscan missionaries worked to Christianize the Indians and to bring about some degree of allegiance to Spanish rule. Some twenty-six thousand Indians had converted at mid-century, many doing so in return for the promise of protection and the advantages of trade. During the latter half of the seventeenth century, however, conflict between the Spanish and English resulted in the virtual elimination of the Spanish and the arrival of English settlers and their African slaves.

During the Spanish era, the Indians had been given sovereignty over their land and freedom from enslavement in return for their souls and their loyalty to Spain. Indians chiefs received horses, swords, fancy clothes, and other symbols of social rank and distinction. This system worked particularly well among the Timucua and Apalachee tribes, where Christian missionaries became an integral part of Indian villages, and Indians were often induced to do the Spaniards' physical labor.

By about 1650, many Indians were becoming restless under this regimen and many others died of European diseases that the Spanish had brought. In 1647, the Apalachees revolted against their Christian brethren in the hope of halting Spanish encroachment into their lives and liberties. Nine years later, the Timucua revolted after the Spanish forced several chiefs to perform physical tasks long considered beneath their dignity. Neither revolt succeeded, although that of the Timucua resulted in many priests leaving their Indian village posts and an end to Spanish gifts.

In 1680 English slave hunters sent their Indian allies out after rival Indians who could be sold as slaves. Most of the remaining Spanish missions closed during this time, while the remaining ones relocated to the relative safety of the area near St. Augustine. The English continued to capture Indians in the south for the slave trade into the early eighteenth century.

In Virginia, the late eighteenth century was marked by the continued depopulation of the Powhatan confederacy. Remaining Indians lived on small reservations on the fringes of colonial settlement, and chiefs served at the pleasure of the colonial government in Jamestown. African slaves in increasing numbers worked in tobacco fields that had once been Indian land. By 1700, only about 1,900 Indians still lived in eastern Virginia, down from nearly seventy thousand when the English first came.

The English and Spanish regard for Indians was starkly different. The English regarded colonization as a business venture in which the Indians were an obstacle to be removed. They seldom recognized Indian land rights but simply claimed for themselves (and the king) all the land described in their royal charter. Except for Pocahontas, they were not much interested in converting Indians to Christianity; many thought that task was a useless endeavor. The Indians in Virginia made one major attempt to resist the English, that of Opechancanough's forces in 1644, and after that failed, the Powhatans were of no social or economic consequence to the colony.

Around 1650, the English began trading with the natives who lived in the Piedmont region, farther to the west. These tribes, which had previously had very little contact with whites, were, like so many others, quickly decimated by disease and warfare. Often battles were fought between rival Indian tribes rather than between English militia and Indians; the English became skilled at pitting tribes against each other. After 1670, much of this activity was conducted from the more recently settled Charles Town (what is now Charleston, South Carolina), where the local economy was based on trade in furs and Indian slaves.

Clearly, no place in the area of English settlement in North America was pleasant for Indians in the late seventeenth century. Regarding colonization as primarily a business venture, the English treated Indians as economic assets for the slave trade, or as obstacles to progress when more land was needed to meet the demands of the ever-increasing number of settlers.

INTERPRETIVE ESSAY
Steven E. Siry

In 1675 the long-standing alliance between the colony of Plymouth and the Wampanoag Indians came to an end. For years advancing colonial settlement had gradually reduced the Indians' landbase. Moreover, the increasing English population had driven away game, which greatly diminished the Indians' fur trade, and the colonists' livestock strayed into Indians' fields, destroying their crops. The Wampanoags were also alarmed at the influence of English culture on Indian children. Many of the tribal *sachems* especially resented the Christian missionaries. Metacom, known to the English as King Philip, supposedly told John Eliot, a leading missionary, that "he cared no more for the white man's gospel than he did for a button on Eliot's coat." For Metacom, who succeeded his father Massasoit as the *sachem* of the Wampanoags, there had also been humiliations at the hands of the English. In 1671 colonial authorities had ordered him to surrender a large stock of guns, to pay a heavy fine, and to accept a treaty acknowledging Wampanoag submission to English law.

The Indians had limited options by the 1670s. They could sell their land to pay off trade debts and become laborers in the colonial settlements, they could move westward into areas controlled by the Five Nations of the Iroquois, or they could create a pan-Indian alliance to launch a war against the colonists. The decision for war was made after Wampanoag braves, allegedly under orders from Metacom, murdered John Sassamon, a Christianized, Harvard-educated Indian informer, though he denied responsibility. In January 1675, the informer had told Plymouth officials that the Wampanoags were planning an attack on colonial settlements. When the informer was murdered and stuffed under pond ice, the Plymouth government arrested and executed three Wampanoags. This action further outraged the Wampanoag Indians, who asserted that the English had violated Wampanoag sovereignty. By the end of the summer, they went to war against the English, who saw the conflict as an opportunity to seize more tribal lands and to subjugate the remaining powerful tribes in southern New England.

At the beginning of the conflict, the Wampanoags successfully carried out several raids on settlements in Plymouth and Massachusetts, and the colonial governments initially failed to create a unified front against the attacks. This led to numerous Algonquin tribes, including the Nipmucs, Narragansetts, Pocumtucks, and Pocassets, becoming allies of the Wampanoags. Indian ambushes occurred in the late summer at Northfield and Whalely. Survivors reported that the Indians had cut off soldiers' heads and put them on poles, had burned captives at the stake, and had hooked a chain into the underjaw of one colonial prisoner and hung him from the bough of a tree.

By December, Metacom's forces had attacked along the New England frontier and destroyed settlements in the entire upper Connecticut River valley. But on December 19, 1675, colonial forces attacked the Narragansetts' refuge, which lay hidden in a swamp in Rhode Island. What ensued has been called the "Great Swamp Fight." Despite suffering heavy losses, the colonial militia set fire to the Narragansett town. Most of the warriors escaped, but many of the noncombatants became casualties, as more than six hundred Narragansett men, women, and children perished in the battle. As Cotton Mather later phrased it, many had been "terribly Barbikew'd." This was one of at least two major battles where the English indiscriminately killed women, children, and old men.

In January 1676 Metacom led Indian forces into winter encampment approximately fifty miles from Albany, New York. Besides about 400 of Metacom's men, there were many hundreds of other Algonquin Indians from southern and northern New England, the largest number being Narragansetts who survived the Great Swamp Fight. Promising weapons, food, clothing, and shelter, Governor Edmund Andros of New York persuaded the Mohawks, always the most aggressive of the Iroquois, and some of their Iroquoian brethren to attack the Algonquins in early February and thus clear New York of this enemy. It was an extremely successful surprise attack. Only 40 of Metacom's 400 men survived, and many of them were badly wounded. The other Algonquins were dispersed. This was the key battle that prevented Metacom from emerging as the primary leader of the Algonquins and from creating a wider Indian alliance. Nevertheless, the war would continue to bear King Philip's name.

Despite the defeats at the Great Swamp Fight and near Albany, Algonquin forces by March 1676 were less than twenty miles from Providence and Boston. Refugees flooded into the coastal areas, profiteering in food supplies developed, and resistance to the colonial drafts became widespread. Nevertheless, the defeat at the hands of the Mohawks had eliminated the Algonquins' ability to attack the major New England towns. Furthermore, in the spring of 1676 the Indians suffered from the spread of diseases and a lack of supplies.

In the summer some Indians moved westward, while others surrendered. Indeed, during King Philip's War, the colonial governments were forced to deal with many Indian prisoners. Authorities in all of the New England colonies executed numerous enemy captives. Viewing the war as a rebellion instead of a war between nations, the English felt that the "rebels" deserved to be executed. Moreover, in such a bloody conflict, the colonists believed the execution of Indians was a just punishment and a good means to ensure the security of the colonial population. In the fall of 1675 Captain Samuel Moseley, described as a former buccaneer from the West Indies, reported the interrogation of a captured Indian woman and that the "aforesaid Indian was ordered to be torn to peeces by Doggs and she was soe dealt with."

But usually Indian prisoners were not killed until they had been given some form of a legal trial. Military commanders, however, sometimes were allowed to execute prisoners without a trial. Furthermore, occasionally private citizens would take the law into their own hands. For example, in Marblehead, Massachusetts, a group of women decapitated two Indian prisoners.

Public pressure could also affect the authorities' actions. At the end of the war, an Indian leader known as Chuff, who was badly wounded, arrived in a small Rhode Island settlement. Because the townspeople felt he had led attacks against Providence, they demanded his execution. The Town Council and the Council of War sentenced Chuff to death and he was soon shot.

Even when the English had no desire to execute captive Indians, the colonists' Indian allies sought their deaths. In April 1676 Pequot warriors captured the Narragansett *sachem* Canonchet. After he was taken to Stonington, the English succumbed to the Connecticut Indians' demand that he be executed. Before his death in front of an English firing squad, Canonchet asserted: "I like it well. I shall die before my heart is soft or I have said anything unworthy of myself."

The colonial authorities also sold numerous captive Indians into bonded servitude or slavery. No record exists of the exact number of Indians involved. But many were sent to slave markets in Spain, the Mediterranean coasts, Virginia, and the West Indies. Some areas, however, believing that North American Indians made poor slaves, refused to purchase them. The governments in Barbados and Jamaica even passed legislation barring their entrance.

Selling prisoners of war into slavery went far beyond the usual treatment. But the practice dated back to the Pequot War of 1637, and a 1641 Massachusetts law allowed the practice if it involved "lawful captives taken in just wars." Since many colonial officials claimed that the Indians were traitorous rebels, they viewed the punishment as just. However, not all the Indians sold into slavery had been hostile to the colonists. For example, in July 1675, soon after an attack on Dartmouth in Plymouth,

160 Indians, who had not participated in the assault, surrendered to colonial authorities when promised amnesty. Nevertheless, all but six of
the Indians were sold into foreign slave markets. In short, sizable profits
made from the slave trade also fostered the practice. A number of the
colonists, however, unsuccessfully opposed the policy. Some had hu-
manitarian concerns, while others wanted to use the captive Indians as
a source of cheap labor in New England. Still other New Englanders
noted that the Indians would continue the war even longer and fight
more fiercely if they knew that slavery would result from defeat.

Using Indian scouts and tactics, colonial militia in early August 1676
attacked Metacom's camp. He escaped, but 173 Indians were killed or
captured. The latter included Metacom's wife and nine-year-old son,
who were subsequently sold into slavery in the West Indies. When Metacom learned of their fates, he declared: "My heart breaks. Now I am
ready to die." On August 12, English forces, guided by one of Metacom's
own men who had turned traitor, ambushed his sleeping camp, and
Metacom was shot through the heart. The militia and their Indian allies
then cut off his head and hands, quartered his body, and hung the parts
in trees. After Metacom's death, sporadic fighting occurred for several
months; a formal treaty, the Peace of Casco, was not signed until April
12, 1678.

A total defeat of the English had been impossible since the start of the
war. Their much larger population, as well as their extensive network of
logistical support from America to Europe, provided the English with a
tremendous advantage over the Indian insurgents. Nevertheless, a stale-
mate might have been achieved if the tribes of southern New England
throughout the war had gained the assistance of the Mohawks or the
Abenakis, a powerful Algonquin tribe in northern New England that had
ties with the French. But without such allies, the Indians of southern
New England were decisively defeated. The Algonquins succumbed to
a two-front war against the English and the Mohawks.

New England experienced elation and relief at the end of King Philip's
War. Yet New Englanders also had to deal with the war's enormous
destruction. Proportional to population, King Philip's War resulted in
more casualties than any other war in American history. New England
lost over 600 men in the fighting, which was close to one-tenth of all
adult males. In less than two years' time, as many as twenty-five hundred colonists were killed out of a total population of approximately
fifty-two thousand people. Thomas Hutchinson, nearly a century later,

claimed that "Every person, almost, [in Massachusetts] lost a relation or near friend." Indeed, King Philip's War was the most destructive war ever fought in New England.

All New England colonies had suffered losses, with the frontier outposts experiencing the greatest destruction. The district of Maine, which had contained thirteen towns and plantations at the beginning of the war, suffered such devastation that it did not recover for half a century. Though New Hampshire suffered very little, Massachusetts experienced extensive losses. Overall, in New England sixteen towns were destroyed or deserted, and another forty towns came under attack. Twenty years after the war, not all of the towns devastated in 1676 had been reestablished. For example, in Connecticut few towns were started in the 1680s, and not until almost 1700 did a major westward advancement resume. When towns were rebuilt, the new communities often were more compact for defensive purposes.

The war had also very negatively affected New England's economy. The fur trade had nearly ended, eight thousand head of cattle had been killed, the import and export trade had often been interrupted, and the fishing industry had suffered a serious decline, as sailors were recruited into the war effort. In addition, the United Colonies (Massachusetts Bay, Plymouth, and Connecticut) asserted that their wartime expenses totaled over £80,000. This led to high taxes. Before 1675 Massachusetts colonists had paid a "country rate" or town levies which were fairly light. But in 1675 the Massachusetts government started using multiple rates that were much higher. These could be paid in money or corn. Not until 1775 in New England did per capita incomes recover their 1675 levels. The pre-1675 norm was not surpassed until after 1815. In part this was because during 1676–1776 a ten-fold increase in population occurred primarily in the area settled before 1676. But the new settlers also often started from "scratch," which had not been the situation before 1676. King Philip's War had destroyed much of the previous generation's investments and placed significant restrictions on westward expansion.

Ironically, the Puritans' campaign against the New England Indians led to the Covenant Chain Conferences of 1677 between the English government and the Five Nations of the Iroquois. These conferences created a frontier line on the west and south between the colonists and the Iroquois that proved to be a solid barrier to colonial expansion. Furthermore, the New England colonies were now bordered on the north by Indian tribes backed by the French. As a result, the New England colonies, which had been very expansionistic before 1675, would remain ter-

ritorially restricted until the American Revolution. In addition, both
Algonquin and Iroquois Indians continued to attack New England's
frontier settlements until the end of the French and Indian War in 1763.
For example, in 1704 Indians again destroyed towns in the Connecticut
River valley that had been reestablished after King Philip's War.

Moreover, due to the many soldiers who served for extended periods,
King Philip's War created America's first enormous problem concerning
veterans. Indeed, in the aftermath of the war, veterans' organizations
were created. The colonial governments usually provided relief to
wounded veterans in the form of a one-time payment. But this could be
supplemented with special privileges, including a tax-exempt status or
the right to collect and keep all fines for violating liquor laws. In addition, some colonial legislatures and some towns provided benefits, especially land grants from areas vacated by the Indians, to survivors of
deceased soldiers and to wounded or unwounded veterans. But not all
were compensated. More than fifty years after the end of King Philip's
War, some veterans or their descendants were still pressuring colonial
legislatures for tracts of land.

The war had also cost many people their homes or businesses. In Massachusetts alone, more than two thousand colonists required assistance.
To assist those in need of help, churches, charitable colonists, and sympathetic Europeans sent various types of aid. In addition, funds were
raised to ransom colonists who had been captured by the Indians. For
example, Mary Rowlandson and her son were ransomed when citizens
in Boston and Portsmouth raised £27.

As a result of King Philip's War, the Algonquin Indians of southern
New England had suffered a devastating defeat. Six thousand Indians,
including most of the Narragansetts, the largest and most powerful tribe
of the region, had died, were enslaved, or were reduced to becoming
hired servants or poor farmers. But some Indians fled to New York,
Virginia, the Susquehanna and Delaware valleys, or Canada as they
sought to preserve their culture and their independence.

The New England colonies supervised all remaining Indians by limi-
ting their daily activities. For example, in Rhode Island, the Indians were
not allowed to gather in substantial numbers, and Rhode Island and
Plymouth placed restrictions on the ownership or carrying of firearms.
In addition, New England authorities assigned the Indians to various
areas. This included the so-called praying Indians. Indeed, the Christian
missionary movement in New England suffered a significant decline during the war. Many of the colonists distrusted the Christian Indians, and

there was reason for some of this distrust. Most of the western Nipmucs, who had been exposed to Christianity for less than five years, had joined the Indian insurgents' uprising. But the colonists did not differentiate among the Christian Indians. Massachusetts authorities rounded up all the Bay Colony's praying Indians and relocated them to wind-swept Deer Island in Boston Harbor. Due to inadequate food, clothing, and shelter, a number of these Indians died during their imprisonment. Yet, numerous Christian Indians, despite all their suffering, remained devoted to their faith.

Four Christian Indian towns were rebuilt in postwar Massachusetts, but these were no longer just for the praying Indians. According to a 1677 law, these towns became reservations for the entire Indian population. But the towns were often headed by *sachems* and the churches headed by other Indians. In this way, the Algonquins, who adopted the European concept of land ownership and many other English ways, also maintained clan boundaries as the principal form of social organization and successfully preserved much of their culture, especially in crafts and trades. In short, these Indians' culture at the end of the 1600s became a combination of Algonquin and English. In the 1700s, however, the Indians increasingly lived more like the English, including their styles of housing. Furthermore, by 1750 Indian languages had largely ceased to be used in New England, as more Native Americans spoke only English.

When King Philip's War ended, colonists commemorated their victory by distributing and displaying throughout New England many bloody reminders of the conflict. For example, colonists from across the region went to Plymouth to view Metacom's head. The colonists also published books and almanacs that listed the dates and provided detailed descriptions of significant wartime events. As the years went by, the descriptions became less detailed, but there remained just one interpretation of the cause of the war: the Indians were to blame.

Before King Philip's War Puritan clergy condemned what they believed was a lack of discipline and numerous manifestations of ungodliness in New England. During the war, New England ministers asserted that Indian victories were indications of God's displeasure with the settlers, and that the defeats inflicted on the Indians indicated a sense of penitence and spiritual regeneration among the colonists. Despite the colonists' victory in King Philip's War, the conflict helped to usher in a tension-filled era in New England. In the postwar period, the dislocations of individuals and groups of people brought by the war adversely affected Puritan congregationalism's rigid discipline that normally was under the control of church and state. Efforts by the church leaders to reverse this trend were in vain. The attitudes created by the uprooted- ness of the war would eventually contribute to the development of the Great Awakening, an extensive religious revival movement in the 1700s.

Besides the religious upheaval of the postwar era, New England's eco- nomic troubles prompted many colonists to become more involved in colonial politics and to challenge traditional authority. In some instances they placed new restrictions on the powers of government officials. Pop- ular concern over government affairs would increase when the Dominion of New England was created in 1686, which for four years brought under one government the colonies of Massachusetts, Connecticut, Plymouth, New Hampshire, Rhode Island, New York, and New Jersey.

In both its short- and long-term effects, King Philip's War had a dra- matic impact on the development of New England. The Indians of the southern part of the region risked total defeat to stop the increasing colonial control over their societies. But the desperate gamble failed. In 1687 a visitor to New England asserted that there was nothing to fear from the Indians for the "last Wars they had with the English . . . have reduced them to a small number." The power of the tribes had been completely shattered, and a legacy of hatred had been created between the Indians and the colonists that would last for generations to come.

SELECTED BIBLIOGRAPHY

Axtell, James. *The Indians' New South: Cultural Change in the Colonial Southeast.* Baton Rouge: Louisiana State University Press, 1997. A study of the impact of the Europeans on the southeastern Indians between 1500 and 1700.

Bourne, Russell. *The Red King's Rebellion: Racial Politics in New England, 1675– 1678.* New York: Oxford University Press, 1990. Extensively covers the background and course of the war.

Calloway, Colin G. *New Worlds for All: Indians, Europeans, and the Remaking of Early America.* Baltimore, MD: Johns Hopkins University Press, 1997. At- tempts to integrate the Indians as important participants in the making of history and the shaping of societies in early America.

Ferling, John E. *A Wilderness of Miseries: War and Warriors in Early America.* West- port, CT: Greenwood Press, 1980. A topical study of war in colonial and Revolutionary America.

Hawke, David Freeman. *Everyday Life in Early America.* New York: Harper and Row, 1988. One chapter provides a brief overview of colonial warfare in the seventeenth century.

Jennings, Francis. *The Invasion of America: Indians, Colonialism, and the Cant of Conquest.* Chapel Hill: University of North Carolina Press, 1975. A revisionist work that portrays the war as an unjustified seizing of native territory by the English colonists.

Josephy, Alvin M., Jr. *The Patriot Chiefs: A Chronicle of American Indian Leadership*. New York: Viking Press, 1961. One chapter covers Metacom's role in the war.

———. *500 Nations: An Illustrated History of North American Indians*. New York: Alfred A. Knopf, 1994. Provides an overview of Indian history to the end of the nineteenth century.

Leach, Douglas E. *Flintlock and Tomahawk: New England in King Philip's War*. New York: W. W. Norton, 1958. Detailed study of the causes, course, and costs of the war.

Lepore, Jill. *The Name of War: King Philip's War and the Origins of American Identity*. New York: Alfred A. Knopf, 1998. Extensively covers certain aspects of the war, such as the experiences of captivity, confinement, and slavery. It also shows how participants and later generations portrayed the war in various types of literature.

Malone, Patrick M. *The Skulking Way of War: Technology and Tactics Among the New England Indians*. Lanham, MD: Madison Books, 1991. Looks at combat in seventeenth-century New England and shows how the Indians' abilities in forest warfare, in combination with their mastery of firearms, made them into fearsome enemies of the English colonists.

Mathews, Lois Kimball. *The Expansion of New England: The Spread of New England Settlement and Institutions to the Mississippi River, 1620–1865*. New York: Russell and Russell, 1962. Originally published in 1909, this book provides information about the war's effect on frontier settlements in New England.

Melvoin, Richard I. *New England Outpost: War and Society in Colonial Frontier Deerfield, Massachusetts*. New York: W. W. Norton, 1989. Shows the impact of King Philip's War on a frontier community.

Millett, Allan R., and Peter Maslowski. *For the Common Defense: A Military History of the United States of America*. Rev. ed. New York: Free Press, 1994. Places King Philip's War within the context of other colonial warfare.

Nash, Gary B. *Red, White, and Black: The Peoples of Early North America*. Third ed. Englewood Cliffs, NJ: Prentice-Hall, 1992. Contains a very concise overview of the war.

Puglisi, Michael J. *Puritans Besieged: The Legacies of King Philip's War in the Massachusetts Bay Colony*. Lanham, NY and London: University Press of America, 1991. A very detailed study of the various costs of the war for the major colony in New England.

Webb, Stephen Saunders. *1676: The End of American Independence*. Syracuse, NY: Syracuse University Press, 1984. Argues that King Philip's War forestalled New England's expansion for almost a century.

9

The Glorious Revolution in America, 1688–1689

INTRODUCTION

After 1660 and the restoration of Charles II to the English throne, American colonies grew more and more restive about political and religious questions. Josias Fendall attempted to oust the Catholic rulers of Maryland in 1660, political dissenters caused trouble in New Jersey in 1672, and William Davyes and John Pate rebelled against Lord Baltimore's absolutism in Maryland in 1676, but they failed and were executed. These were fairly minor outbursts of colonial assertiveness; of far more concern was Bacon's Rebellion in Virginia in 1676.

The most serious challenge to colonial authority in the seventeenth century, Bacon's Rebellion came about in the midst of an effort by prominent Virginians in London to obtain a royal charter that would guarantee certain rights, including that of land ownership and taxation only with the consent of those being taxed. Virginians wanted "the same liberties and privileges as Englishmen in England" (Clark, p. 243). Bacon's Rebellion, which complicated the charter effort, was ironic in that the rebels were making almost the same requests of the Virginia elite as the elite were making in London. Bacon and his supporters demanded protection from Indians, lower taxes, and rectification of local grievances.

Nathaniel Bacon's father had withdrawn his son from Cambridge Uni-

King James II of England was overthrown in the Glorious Revolution.
(Reproduced from the Collections of the Library of Congress.)

versity for having "broken into some extravagancies" (Clark, p. 244); after the young Bacon's arrival in Virginia, he was suspected of atheistic tendencies. He wanted to fight Indians, who were causing trouble on the frontier near his Henrico County plantation, but the governor would not sanction an Indian war. Bacon led an expedition in defiance of the governor and at different times found himself fighting both the Indians and the governor's troops. But he had a large following, and had he not died suddenly of natural causes in October 1676, his movement might have gone much further. After Bacon's death, the governor's forces easily subdued the rebellion.

Even before Bacon died, his movement prompted the convening of an assembly at Jamestown to discuss a variety of colonial grievances. Out of the assembly, at which Bacon himself had no particular influence, came several reforms, including one that allowed all freeholders to vote for members of the House of Burgesses, the Virginia colonial assembly. Another reform removed the tax-exempt status of council members. Soon afterward the council (the upper house of the colonial legislature) repealed the laws passed at the Jamestown assembly, and London sent over a team of royal commissioners and later a new royal governor to strengthen imperial authority over Virginia.

In New England, after years of contentiousness between England and the colonies, James II united all the New England colonies with New York and New Jersey into the Dominion of New England and appointed Sir Edmund Andros as governor in 1686. Andros, who had served as governor of New York, ruled with considerable more authority than the New Englanders wanted. He enforced the Navigation Acts, regularized colonial administration, and strengthened colonial defenses. James had decreed that no colonial assembly should meet nor should towns be permitted to hold town meetings. Andros's ardent Anglicanism offended Puritan leaders, and as his enforcement of trade regulations brought economic decline, moderate merchants joined with the Puritans to oppose the governor.

In England, James II had succeeded his brother, Charles II, in 1685. As king, James determined to advance the cause of Catholicism, out of favor in England since the reign of Henry VIII (1509–47). In his first years on the throne, James managed to antagonize the Church of England in several ways. He established an ecclesiastical court, the Commissioners of Ecclesiastical Causes, that was designed to restrain the authority of Anglican priests and promote the appointment of Catholics to official posts. He issued two Declarations of Indulgence, seen as a ploy to legitimize Catholicism.

One of the early actions of the Commissioners of Ecclesiastical Causes was to suspend the bishop of London, Henry Compton, who also had jurisdiction over Anglicanism in the colonies. Compton had become bishop of London in 1675 and was also a member of the Council of Trade and Plantations, which had assumed control of colonial affairs the year before. As a member of the Lords of Trade, Compton worked to promote the Anglican Church in the colonies. Based on reports of the neglectful attitude of the colonists toward the church, Compton increased the authority of ministers in their parishes and ordered parishes to provide better financial support for their ministers. In 1679, Compton stipulated that all Anglican ministers bound for the colonies must obtain a certificate of appointment from him, and by 1685, the bishop and his certified ministers had taken over many other ecclesiastical powers in the colonies.

Suspended early in James II's reign for not disciplining Anglican ministers who had been critical of the king, Compton saw his duties given over to a royal commission that the king could easily influence. Seven other Anglican bishops, including the bishop of Canterbury, who had publicly challenged the constitutionality of the second Declaration of Indulgence, were sent to the Tower of London to await trial on charges of sedition. After a month, the trial was held and the seven were acquitted.

On June 30, 1688, the same day as the acquittal of the bishops, a group of prominent but aggrieved subjects of the Crown, including Bishop Compton, set the Glorious Revolution in motion. They invited William of Orange to come from the Netherlands and reign in England as William III with his wife, Mary, the oldest daughter of James II, who would become Mary II. Since James II's consort, whose name was also Mary, had just given birth to a son and heir, time was of the essence, and William was asked to come sooner rather than later.

In the early fall of 1688, William announced his intent to go to England to maintain Protestantism and a "free and lawful Parliament." He and his troops landed in England on November 5 and reached London within six weeks, forcing James to flee into exile in France. Englishmen in general rejoiced, although some were uneasy about the rapid changes occurring in their hallowed institutions. When a Scottish bishop rebuked a preacher for an enthusiastic pro-William sermon, the preacher replied, "He [who] is afraid of a fart will never stand thunder" (quoted in Lovejoy, p. 226).

Parliament met in January 1689 and passed measures that implemented the political agenda of the Glorious Revolution. The Mutiny Act, the Toleration Act, the Bill of Rights, and the Corporation Act were among the acts passed, and for the American colonies, the Corporation Act was especially important, since it restored city and borough charters that James had suspended, including those in New England. As thankful as Parliament was to have William on the throne, the new monarch was not entirely supportive of what Parliament was trying to do. He and some of his supporters were reluctant to surrender some of their authority and see the country move in the direction of republicanism. Many English moderates had liked James II's imposition of the Dominion of New England, because it made for more effective colonial administration and centralized imperial authority.

After news of the Glorious Revolution reached Boston in early 1689, Andros's opponents armed themselves and overthrew the governor, jailing him and most of his officials. War with the French suspended colonial administration until 1691, when Massachusetts received a new charter from London. This charter provided for an elected assembly as well as an elected council, but the governor, who had veto power, was a Crown appointee. All of this struck a compromise between the virtually independent Massachusetts of pre-1686 days and the severely constricted colony under the Dominion of New England government. The new charter also brought Massachusetts into rough conformity with the other colonies. It also brought an end to the waning Plymouth colony by merging it with Massachusetts. Plymouth had been in economic distress for many years, and the incorporation into the larger colony was not resisted.

Not long before the Glorious Revolution, the Virginia House of Burgesses petitioned James II to recall the colonial governor, Lord Howard of Effingham. James was overthrown before he could act on the petition, but William was sympathetic and placed royal authority in the hands of the lieutenant governor Francis Nicholson. Lord Howard, who was in England when all of this was happening, did not return to Virginia, and relations between the assembly and Nicholson were peaceful

In Maryland, a dissident named John Coode raised a force in 1689, seized public buildings and Lord Baltimore's plantation, and set up an interim government that excluded Catholics. Coode had been a Protestant activist well before the Glorious Revolution. In 1681, he and a friend, Josias Fendall, had tried to stir up sentiment against Catholics in Maryland. They were arrested, thrown in jail, and tried in November 1681 on charges of mutiny and sedition. Coode was found not guilty, but Fendall was convicted, fined forty thousand pounds of tobacco, and banished from the colony.

Coode's government, in power after 1689, was not universally popular, although it legitimized itself with a convention in 1690. Many Marylanders thought it oppressive (any opponent to the government was deemed an opponent to William III), and even Coode said he favored a new royal government sent from London. Coode's past association with troublemakers like Fendall did not help his cause either, nor did assertions that he was using his power to enrich himself. Lord Baltimore, meanwhile, worked hard to regain his authority in Maryland, offering amnesty to Coode and consenting to have a Protestant governor appointed, but London was not sympathetic. William III appointed Lionel Copley as royal governor and sent him to Maryland to establish the Anglican Church there as well as a fairly typical colonial administration and government. Under Copley, who died in 1694, and Francis Nicholson, who replaced him, Maryland returned to a semblance of normality.

Similarly, in New York, the local militia heard about the Glorious Revolution and the revolt in Massachusetts in the spring of 1689 and seized the royal fort from English troops. A rebel-formed group, the Committee of Safety, served as an interim government and appointed one of its members Jacob Leisler commander in chief of the colony. The members of the committee proclaimed their loyalty to William III and Mary and to Leisler, a German merchant who had never been part of the colony's ruling elite. All of this offended a number of Dutch landowners from the Albany area and socially prominent Englishmen from the New York City area, who also praised William III and Mary II but considered Leisler an illegitimate leader.

Leisler tried to get William III and Mary II to recognize his government by sending over personal representatives to lobby the court and Parliament, but those he sent did not serve him well. One of his agents, Joost Stoll, a liquor merchant, spent most of his time making business deals for himself, and the other, Matthew Clarkson, worked to get himself appointed to a royal position in the colonial government. Leisler's government, unlike those in Maryland and Massachusetts, was not recognized in London. Instead, William III appointed a new colonial government headed by Henry Slaughter, an English military officer. Slaughter came to New York in January 1691 expecting chaos in the colony. There was no chaos, but there was the strong-willed Leisler, who battled with Slaughter for authority from the time the new governor stepped on shore.

Leisler was suspicious of nearly everyone around him, and when two companies of English troops showed up, he was convinced that a conspiracy against his rule had formed. In March, Leisler and his forces dug in at a fortress in New York City; the British troops challenged him, and a showdown was at hand. Firing from both sides resulted in the deaths of several men. Eventually, Leisler surrendered the fort, and Slaughter immediately arrested him, marking the end of the rebellion. Leisler and nine accomplices stood trial at the end of March; in early May, Leisler was convicted of "traitorously levying war" against William III and Mary and "feloniously murdering" one Josias Brown, a man killed in a skirmish during Leisler's resistance. Seven of Leisler's nine accomplices were also found guilty, and two weeks after the verdict was announced, Leisler and his guilty accomplices were hanged.

Although rebellions like Leisler's and improvised governments like Coode's suggest that the Glorious Revolution brought substantial changes to the politics of the colonies, English authorities did not see it this way. William III tolerated the renewal of colonial autonomy because the North American colonies were not particularly important to him. The king continued to assert that he had ultimate authority over the colonies, but that it was exercised through Parliament rather than directly. And members of Parliament believed that they could alter acts of colonial assemblies at their will. Thus the Glorious Revolution did not fundamentally change the relationship between England and its colonies in America.

Perhaps the Glorious Revolution more significantly affected colonial commerce. The Council of Trade and Plantations continued to exert some authority over the colonies, and a new Navigation Act in 1696 put stricter controls on commerce, in part by establishing Admiralty Courts, which sat in judgment of trade violations in the colonies. A new agency, the Board of Trade and Plantations, was created to oversee colonial affairs, but it was hampered by other parliamentary agencies, such as the War Office and the secretary of state for the Southern Department, both of which also bore some responsibility for colonial administration. Enforcement of commercial regulations was inefficient, however, and colonists were more inclined to be law-abiding because of the danger posed by England's rivals, France and Spain.

INTERPRETIVE ESSAY
P. D. Swiney

The revolution of 1688 in England is referred to as the "Glorious" Revolution because it created a constitutional settlement. Parliament, the representative assembly, became the sovereign power in English government. The Glorious Revolution in the American colonies was marked by three rebellions—in Massachusetts, New York, and Maryland. Rear-rangements of power occurred in all the colonies, but with unforeseen and unexpected consequences. The colonists had been forcibly reminded that they were Englishmen, part of a growing empire. The Glorious Rev-olution in America was their declaration of indifference; that what was good for the British empire was not necessarily of interest or concern to the colonies. The colonists would move to defend the existing arrange-ments and practices that were of benefit to the individual settlements that dotted North America.

The restoration of the Stuart monarchy in 1660 was yet another at-tempt to provide stability and coherence to a government and society rent by religious, civil, and political strife. Contention between central-izing royal power and local government had torn England for decades. Parliament, the representative assembly of wealthy gentry and nobility, had struggled for supremacy with the autocratic Stuart kings. A growing national identification with Protestantism had led to a growing loathing of Catholics, and dissenting sects among the Protestants proposed radical revision of the distribution of land, property, and power. After the 1658 death of Oliver Cromwell, the Lord Protector, negotiations opened to bring back the heir of the beheaded Charles I. Charles II returned to England grateful to those who had shown loyalty to him in more than a decade of exile. Some of this gratitude would manifest itself in gen-erous grants of land in the colonies of North America.

Those colonies already in existence had watched developments in En-gland with considerable anxiety. The most successful of the colonies, Massachusetts Bay, had been founded and populated primarily by Pu-ritans. As the Puritans in England had led the opposition to Charles I, rebelled against him, and executed him, it is understandable that Puritan colonies would view the accession of his son with considerable trepi-dation.

The change in government would require all the extant colonies to confirm their colonial charters with the new king. Only Virginia was a royal colony, with a royal governor appointed by the king. Virginia also had the House of Burgesses, a representative assembly, but the Burgesses were property holders, and only property holders could elect them. Maryland was a proprietary colony, founded as a haven for English Catholics by the Catholic Lord Baltimore. As proprietor, Lord Baltimore held title to all the land in his colony and could arrange the government as he saw fit. Massachusetts Bay Colony was a special case: a religious movement masquerading as a stock company. The original settlers/ stockholders had migrated to Massachusetts to be a "city on a hill"— a moral example to the Church of England to inspire it to reform. Massachusetts society and government had been organized around the Puritan version of the Church of England—Calvinist in theology, congregationalist in organization. Congregations existed independently of one another and called their own ministers. But very early, Massachusetts had extended participation in its General Court, or representative assembly, to all endorsed Church members. The governor of the colony was elected, yet the clergy was formally excluded from political affairs. This arrangement, peculiar as it may seem, was carried to a number of smaller settlements: Connecticut, Rhode Island, Providence Plantations, New Haven Plantation, and New Hampshire. None of these foundations had legal existence under the new regime.

The king's government in London was aware that political arrangements in the colonies were somewhat irregular, but settlements after years of uncertainty in the government in England claimed the major attention of the king's ministers. After persistent petitions by agents sent by the colonists, the king made his dispositions over a period of several years. Massachusetts could continue under its original charter—for the present. Rhode Island and Providence Plantation were to combine, but preserve their government. Connecticut and New Haven were to do the same. New Hampshire was chartered as a separate colony. Maine would be under the authority of Massachusetts. Virginia was denied her claim to territory on her southern border; it would become part of a large grant to a group of the king's closest advisors, as proprietors. They graciously christened their new enterprise Carolina, named after the king. After a successful war against the Dutch, major commercial rivals of England, the king would grant the acquired Dutch territories in the colonies to his brother, the Duke of York, who would then name it for himself—New York. The dual colonies of Jersey were awarded to separate proprietors, creating East and West Jersey. All the new colonies were expected to tolerate other Protestant sects (of which there were a considerable number) and form some variety of a representative assembly to levy taxes. In 1680, Charles discharged an old debt by granting an enormous tract of land to William Penn, a prominent and wealthy member of the unorthodox and disturbing Quaker sect. As proprietor, Penn could rule as he pleased; he was pleased to found a colony for dissenting religious minorities, and constructed an unusually liberal frame of government.

Pennsylvania, after some bumpy adjustments, arrived at a consensual procedure in its assembly and became known as the Best Poor Man's Country.

Unfortunately, Charles's ignorance of colonial geography was as great as his largesse. Not only did his generous grants to friends and supporters collide, but the legal position of the settlers already in possession was jeopardized. The proprietors of New York, East and West Jersey, and the Carolinas proposed to sell these lands as a profit-making venture. Some wished to experiment with forms of government. None would follow any predictable pattern, thereby making administration from London more difficult. London was becoming more interested in the colonies as possibilities for increased revenue. Some of the laws from the Cromwell era were retained as part of a grand imperial design. The Navigation Acts were supposed to curtail trade among the colonies at increased profit to the mother country. They required all English shipments to be carried on English ships, with an English crew. Contracting with carriers offering the most favorable terms was not permitted. All colonial exports and imports were to pass through England, with the accompanying duties and customs paid. Certain highly desirable products of the colonies, "enumerated goods" named by law, were to go only to England, to provide her with a monopoly on desirable exports.

The colonies were not at all fond of the Navigation Acts. They had evaded them and violated them and become proficient smugglers under Cromwell, and they were ready to do so again under Charles II. As the expected revenue fell short of expectations, a special committee of the Privy Council, the Lords of Trade, was created in 1675 to assist in the enforcement of the Navigation Acts. The king's brother, James, Duke of York, was particularly interested in consolidating and streamlining administration of the colonies, and he sponsored a major realignment of government. In 1684, Massachusetts's original charter was revoked, and various other New England colonies lost their patents to confer land titles and organize governments. The plan was to combine all the northern colonies with the administration of New York, making the Dominion of New England. A similar plan was bruited for the southern colonies.

Unfortunately, the creation of the Dominion of New England coincided with the death of Charles II and his brother's accession to the throne. James II's province of New York automatically became a royal colony when he became king, but the orphaned colonies of New England did not learn of their consolidation with New York for months. James was busy securing his throne in the face of bitter opposition to his conversion to Catholicism, and outright rebellion from Charles II's illegitimate (but Protestant) son. In 1686, Sir Edmund Andros was dispatched to administer a sullen Dominion of New England.

Sir Edmund was a soldier and courtier who had already served as governor of the king's province of New York. He was well acquainted with the sectional rivalries between the Albany frontier, which held a monopoly on the fur trade, and the port on Manhattan Island, which was rapidly acquiring a monopoly on regional shipping. The largest population was on Long Island, nonconformist from the dissenting Puritans. After twenty years of English occupation, the Dutch inhabitants had made some adjustment, but increasing English settlement had brought new tensions among Quakers, Anglicans, Lutherans, Dutch Reformed, and Puritans who counted half a dozen nationalities among these congregations, a not uncommon circumstance found in any port.

The New York assembly had been suspended in 1685 by James II, now king of England, and other regional assemblies were dissolved or relegated to local government business only. Andros was to govern with the aid of an appointed council. The suspiciously modest revenues from these thriving areas would be devoted to defense of the English empire in America, chiefly on the vulnerable New York border with French Canada.

Andros proposed to administer the dominion from Boston, and he also intended to institute observance of the English national church in the center of dissent from that church. The imposition of a tax, without the consent of the dissolved General Court, evoked bitter protest from the Puritans. But Andros's attempt to put the dominion on a self-supporting basis by charging fees to reconfirm land titles granted by the defunct previous charter, plus collection of quit rents, a yearly charge for the land already purchased, was more than the Puritans could abide. Increase Mather, a prominent member of an eminent ministerial dynasty, was dispatched in 1688 to London to represent to the king Massachusetts's grievances. When he arrived there, Mather found a capital seething with anti-Catholic sentiment. The king had replaced royal officials with Catholic adherents (including the Lords of Trade), had issued a Declaration of Indulgence (or tolerance) for dissident sects, which was widely perceived as a means of reintroducing Catholicism to England, and had capped his folly by producing a male Catholic heir. Within six months England had embarked on its Glorious Revolution. James II's Protestant firstborn, Mary, was married to a leading Protestant statesman in Europe, William of Orange. Parliament invited them to defend England from James's encroaching Catholicism. William landed with an army in November 1688, James fled to France in December, and by February William and Mary accepted Parliament's offer of the throne of England and were crowned in April 1689. A profound change in England's political system had occurred in a breathless (and bloodless) six months.

Word of these dizzying events came sporadically and late to the colonies. By the time news of William's invasion had arrived, he and Mary had accepted the throne. By the time the colonies heard of the change of monarchs, they had been crowned. Announcement of their coronation arrived six weeks later, but the Dominion of New England no longer existed. On April 18, leading Puritans of Boston, backed by a mob of excited Bostonians, arrested Governor Edmund Andros and other royal officials, as agents of the discarded King James. A Council of Safety was formed, chiefly of members of the former charter government. As word spread of Massachusetts's action, other portions of the dominion followed suit, and New England fragmented back into the colonies of Connecticut, Rhode Island, Plymouth, and Massachusetts Bay.

Andros's deputy in New York, Francis Nicholson, was in a peculiar position. Word of Massachusetts's Glorious Revolution had come far more quickly than England's. Indeed, Nicholson had received word of William and Mary's accession in March, but he had not proclaimed it. Massachusetts had successfully challenged the origin of the authority Nicholson held. While Nicholson waited for some instruction from London and warned Albany to expect an attack from the French, the divisions in New York society manifested themselves.

At the end of May 1689, the commander of the militia, Jacob Leisler, seized Fort James, the fortress of New York City. Rather than confront him (and the large portion of militia at his back) Nicholson sailed for England in June. Upon his departure, Leisler proclaimed the coronation of William III and Mary II and declared his securing of the Anglo-Dutch colony of New York for a Dutch king of England.

In Maryland, a similar set of circumstances occurred. Lord Baltimore had been in England since 1684. The council appointed to govern in his absence made two fatal errors: It dismissed the assembly for two consecutive sessions, and it made Maryland conspicuous in its lack of support for the new king and queen. The council may have regretted the departure of the Catholic James, but the majority of the population in this Catholic proprietor's colony was staunchly Protestant. John Coode seized the opportunity and led a rebellion in 1689 on behalf of a Protestant Association against the autocratic Catholic proprietor. Having seized power, Coode called an increasingly uneasy representative assembly to proclaim William and Mary sovereigns of England and Maryland's loyalty to them. These three rebellions, one reputedly against Catholic tyranny and all citing defense of representative government, were not precisely what they proclaimed themselves.

By no stretch of the twentieth-century imagination can these assemblies be considered "representative" in the sense of considering the interests of the entire population. English political institutions had been carried to the colonies without the accompanying social hierarchies to support them. In England, local government was administered, and representatives sent to Parliament, by the land-owning elite. Political authority was supported by social status, which was based on the holding of land. The longer the land was held by a single family, the higher their social status and political influence. Even the townsmen based status on generations of occupancy, accompanied by wealth. Political power was divided, and local government administered, by these long-dominant families, their allies, and their kin.

But in America, a similar political structure was transplanted without the centuries of land tenure dominance. Many a "new man" made a fortune in the colonies, and in the colonies it was wealth that conferred social status. The presumption of political power that accompanied social status developed in a different pattern. Land was far easier to come by in the colonies, and wealth could quickly accumulate without large tracts of land. The dominant men of the local governments, who sent certain of their number to the assemblies, might not have been accepted as the elite in England, but they were certainly the elite of the colonies.

But in a social structure that creates a self-defined elite, a certain number will predictably be excluded from what they consider their just portion of political power and the accompanying appointments in government where money was made. This was a contributing factor in Jacob Leisler's seizure of Fort James in New York. Leisler himself was a member of the second rank of the Dutch hierarchy who had submitted to English rule. Leisler and his supporters had failed to achieve the highest positions available in the new English administration. Some Dutch had quickly accommodated themselves to English rule and had become a part of the ruling coterie in the English administration of New York, with the accompanying monetary rewards. The Dutch community, still in the majority after twenty years of English rule, was deeply divided among political factions based in kinship networks that were in a continual state of flux. These wealthy families were accustomed to apportioning political power among themselves. Leisler had arrived in New Amsterdam just before it surrendered to the English and had married into a political faction that did not flourish in the duke of York's government.

Leisler's seizure of power was precisely that—an attempt to move himself, and the factions backing him, to a more prominent place in local government. A Committee of Safety called delegates from various settlements in New York and proclaimed Leisler commander in chief. Under this title, Leisler set about dismantling the former government. He was blocked somewhat by Albany, which supported King William but also sustained an ongoing enmity with its downstream rival. Albany simply ignored Leisler's command. A letter sent from the Privy Council addressed to Nicholson stated, "and in his absence such as for the time being take care for preserving the peace and administering the laws," which was all Leisler needed to proclaim himself deputy governor. He ruled as ultimate authority in New York for two years, with large portions of opposing factions, both in the city and up the Hudson Valley to Albany, jailed, exiled, or silenced. However, Leisler was not capable of ceding the power he had coveted for so long. When the duly appointed royal governor arrived from England in 1691, Leisler initially refused to surrender the fort. When he did so, he found himself in chains, accused of treason. The opposing factions rushed to fill the vacancies in government left by Liesler's adherents and pressed for a trial for treason. After a long and contentious legal process, Leisler and his son-in-law were condemned to death. The death penalty was not uncommon in Dutch practice, but death sentences were almost always commuted. The opposition's insistence on his execution sowed permanent bitter divisions in the ruling families of the province of New York.

Maryland's rebellion had similar antecedents. It was a proprietary colony—all the land was owned by Lord Baltimore and the Calvert family and was sold to settlers for profit. Maryland, like Pennsylvania, had been founded as a haven for a persecuted minority, the English Catholics. But Catholicism had been viewed in England as a form of treason for over a century, and Lord Baltimore's haven for Catholics was quickly settled by a majority of Protestants. Instead of the complex divisions that characterized New York politics, Maryland featured a proprietary party, composed of the proprietor, his Council, members of his administration, and all their marital and political allies. The proprietary party kept an iron grip on lucrative government places, and Catholicism, or kinship, seemed the only entry.

An overwhelmingly Protestant majority vastly outnumbered the proprietary party. Unfortunately, Lord Baltimore confirmed every English Protestant prejudice about the equation of Catholicism and tyranny through raising taxes, tobacco price cuts, monopolies awarded to the proprietor's party, and the abolition of the head right system (an easy way to obtain land grants by bringing settlers into the colony; a number of acres was awarded per head). His greatest error, the one that would cost him his government, was the exclusion of Protestant politicians from any advancement in his government. In 1684 Lord Baltimore sailed for England to defend both his charter and his boundary, disputed by the new colony of Pennsylvania. While he was gone, his deputies repeatedly dismissed a defiant and angry General Assembly. In 1689, news of a Protestant prince ascending the English throne was a gift to the disgruntled Protestants of Maryland. While the council declined to proclaim and swear allegiance to the new monarchs, the antiproprietary party was organizing a Protestant Association to declare William and Mary. However, these "associators" had been ringleaders in repeated insurrections long before any change in the monarchy. Charles II and James II had repeatedly upheld the proprietor's regime. William would not be so supportive of a Catholic dissident.

In July 1689, John Coode's armed force seized the capital, St. Mary's, and convened an assembly. In September, it proclaimed King William III and Queen Mary II. In 1690, the rebels sailed for England to confront Lord Baltimore. The new government found in favor of the rebels, Baltimore lost the government of his colony (but not ownership of the land), and Maryland gained a royally appointed governor. The Catholics in Maryland, their former haven and hegemony, were relegated to the status of Catholics in the mother country—fined, disenfranchised, sidelined.

Massachusetts was again an exceptional case. Once the hated Andros was incarcerated, the Council of Safety tried to reestablish the original charter government and recalled its last elected governor to office. But Massachusetts was divided against itself—though many hoped for the restoration of the original charter, where political structures were intertwined with religious position, not all were confident that such a restoration was possible, or even desirable. The fervor that had sent thirty thousand Puritans to a wilderness to create a godly society had waned in the intervening half century. Some were troubled at the equivocal legal position of the colony. Andros could be accused of little but attempting to enforce imperial policy; the same independent spirit, which had resisted him, resisted the new government that rested on such tenuous authority. For three long years, there was no clear central authority in Massachusetts. Andros was returned to England, accompanied by more agents for the Massachusetts colony. Increase Mather had been pleading, cajoling, and lobbying in London since 1688, and his advocates and advisors convinced him that the new king would not tolerate the self-government built into the old charter. The General Court—the representative assembly that had governed the colony since its founding—was restored. But its composition would be permanently altered by the decision to extend the franchise to property holders, rather than members of the church. The king appointed the governor. Massachusetts was no longer God's "city on a hill"; it was another royal colony of North America. But the self-regard that had established the colony as the province of God's elect would not bend readily to imperial imperatives.

By 1696, all the colonies had royally appointed governors. New York gained a representative assembly populated largely by the competing, jealous factions that harbored the residual enmity from Leisler's rebellion. The proprietary families of Maryland and Pennsylvania retained land titles to their colonies until the revolution, but the governments were no longer in their control. Voting privileges in all the colonies were standardized.

The Glorious Revolution in America served, in the long run, to undermine seriously the ties between England and her North American colonies. From the English viewpoint, two laws enacted in 1696 to support and enforce the Navigation Acts would streamline administration, communication, and control of the colonies, thereby increasing English trade and English power. However, avoidance and later defiance of these two provisions would increase the distance between imperial and colonial objectives.

The Board of Trade was created to oversee government and administration in the colonies. It functioned as a clearinghouse for all kinds of colonial affairs, dispatching colonial legislation, customs documents, and military reports to the appropriate offices in the British government for review. It was also an advisory panel for the Privy Council, which made all appointments of colonial officers.

Parliament also found it necessary to extend jurisdiction to vice admiralty courts for violations of the Navigation Acts. Trial by a jury of their peers convicted woefully few smugglers in the North American colonies. The vice admiralty courts established in those colonies could circumvent that problem, as they had no juries. But the law establishing the vice admiralty courts did not eliminate jury trials, and therefore colonial juries continued to acquit their smuggling peers.

In 1701, the Society for the Propagation of the Gospel was founded to convey Anglican missionaries to North America. Only Virginia had established the state Church of England as the state church of Virginia. Some partial establishment (payment of a tax to support the "established," or government-endorsed, religion) had been made in some sectors of New York, Maryland, and North and South Carolina. The other colonies had been founded by, or on behalf of, religious dissenters who formed the bulk of the colonial population. As more colonial officials and administrators came to the colonies, they brought their Anglicanism with them, contributing to an increasingly diverse religious observance.

Also in 1701, the cultural and economic differences in the northern and southern portions of Carolina were recognized, and their division become formal. The following year, East and West Jersey were united.

The unexpected consequence of the Glorious Revolution in the colonies was the echo of parliamentary sovereignty found in the colonial assemblies. As Parliament triumphed at home, so did the colonial assemblies in America. London's neglect of the colonies and absorption in European affairs that led to colonial autonomy in the seventeenth century would permit the disregard of imperial decrees in the eighteenth. Colonial assemblies repeatedly refused to post their militias, or spend their money, to aid other colonies—Virginia, Maryland, Massachusetts, and Pennsylvania all refused royal directives in the first decade of the 1700s. Whenever war broke out between England and France, the colonies were expected to strike at French Canada. Wartime expenses were a burden to each of the colonies; in matters of defense, the colonies were on their own. Paper money issued in the wake of various wars by various colonial governments to pay their local debt was a continual problem for both the local economy and the local government. This circumstance would lead to serious repercussions at the conclusion of the Seven Years' War (known in America as the French and Indian War) in 1763, when London decided to station an English army permanently in North America. Colonists who had managed their own defense (and the accompanying financial burden) for decades were not at all interested in paying for the maintenance of a standing army. The protests over taxation imposed by Parliament would lead to the revolution.

Colonial assemblies, by the "power of the purse" regularly expressed their displeasure with imperial administration by declining to fund the royal officials' salaries. One such dispute is best known as the *Zenger* case, in which newspaper editor John Peter Zenger of New York was charged in 1740 with sedition for supporting the New York Assembly in its dispute with governor. A jury of sympathetic New Yorkers acquitted him. This case is often held up as an early freedom of the press case, because Zenger argued that he could not be publishing treasonous material if it could be proven true. However, it is more accurately an illustration of the power of the colonial legislatures a half century after the Glorious Revolution. Despite the intermittent desire of the imperial government to increase and centralize control over the American colonies, the refusal of the local legislatures to obey instruction and even to pay the salaries of royal officials demonstrates that the colonists viewed their assemblies as "mini-Parliaments," and the Glorious Revolution had made Parliament sovereign. The insistence on the powers of their local governments would lead the colonists to their own revolution in 1776.

SELECTED BIBLIOGRAPHY

Arch, Stephen Carl. " The Glorious Revolution and the Rhetoric of Puritan History." *Early American Literature* 27 (1992): 61–74. How the Puritans convinced themselves their rebellion was not treasonous.

Archdeacon, Thomas J. *New York City, 1664–1710: Conquest and Change.* Ithaca, NY: Cornell University Press, 1976. A population analysis and study of popular politics, with emphasis on Dutch-English conflict.

Bailyn, Bernard. "Politics and Social Structure in Virginia." In *Seventeenth Century American: Essays in Colonial History*, edited by James M. Smith. New York: W. W. Norton, 1959. How fluid social mobility affected the allotment of political power.

Bonomi, Patricia U. *A Factious People: Politics and Society in Colonial New York.* New York: Columbia University Press, 1971. A lucid untangling of colonial New York political rivalries and alliances over an extensive period.

Clark, J. C. D. *The Language of Liberty.* Cambridge, Eng.: Cambridge University Press, 1994. A recent work that analyzes the themes of religion and law in the political discourse between England and America between 1660 and 1832.

Craven, Wesley Frank. *The Colonies in Transition: 1660–1713.* New York: Harper and Row, 1968. A thorough narrative of the crucial period bracketing the Glorious Revolution.

Greene, Jack. *The Quest for Power: The Lower Houses of Assembly in the Southern Royal Colonies 1689–1776.* Chapel Hill: University of North Carolina Press, 1963. How the lower assemblies achieved the upper hand.

————. "Metropolis and Colonies: Changing Patterns of Constitutional Conflict in the Early Modern British Empire, 1607–1763." In *Negotiated Authorities: Essays in Colonial Political and Constitutional History*. Charlottesville: University Press of Virginia, 1994. The conflict between British imperial policy and colonial interests.

Hall, Michael G., Lawrence H. Leder, and Michael G. Kammen, eds. *The Glorious Revolution in America: Documents on the Colonial Crisis of 1689* . Chapel Hill: University of North Carolina Press, 1964. A documentary chronicle of events in New England, New York, and Maryland.

James, Sidney V. *Colonial Rhode Island: A History*. New York: Charles Scribner's Sons, 1975. An enjoyable explanation of why Rhode Island is known as "the land of the otherwise-minded."

Kammen, Michael. "The Causes of the Maryland Revolution of 1689." *Maryland Historical Magazine* (December 1960): 293–333. Poor policy of the Calverts led to popular support for a small, ambitious group of opponents to proprietary rule.

————. *Colonial New York*. New York: Charles Scribner's Sons, 1975. Leisler's rebellion in a comprehensive context.

Lovejoy, David S. *The Glorious Revolution in America*. New York: Harper and Row, 1972. A comprehensive study emphasizing the colonies as part of the British empire.

Miller, Perry. *The New England Mind: From Colony to Province*. Cambridge: Harvard University Press, 1953. An interesting history by the premier authority on Puritan society. Any study of colonial New England must begin with Perry Miller.

Sewall, Samuel. *The Diary and Life of Samuel Sewall*. Edited by Mel Yazawa. New York: Bedford Books, 1998. The events in Boston as recounted by a prominent participant.

Sosin, Jack M. *English America and the Revolution of 1688*. Lincoln: University of Nebraska Press, 1982. The impact of the Glorious Revolution on American political structures.

Stout, Harry O. *The New England Soul: Preaching and Religious Culture in Colonial New England*. New York: Oxford University Press, 1986. A study drawn from sermons that demonstrates the strong influence of Puritanism in politics.

Ver Steeg, Clarence L. *The Formative Years 1697–1763*. New York: Hill and Wang, 1964. The transition from English colonies to American provinces.

This nineteenth-century engraving illustrates one of the judicial proceedings in the Salem witch trials of 1692. (Reproduced from the Collections of the Library of Congress.)

The Salem Witch Trials, 1692

INTRODUCTION

The witch trials of Salem Village, Massachusetts (March to September 1692) were America's most notorious episode of witchcraft hysteria. The belief in witchcraft was carried to colonial America from Europe, where thousands had been executed as witches in the two centuries before 1650. The Salem incident began when two young girls in the household of Reverend Samuel Parris began to behave oddly. One of the girls was Reverend Parris's daughter, Betty. She was nine years old. The other girl was eleven-year-old Abigail Williams, Betty Parris's cousin.

Apparently, the girls had been feeling guilty for dropping an egg in a glass and looking at it in the style of crystal-ball gazing, a forbidden behavior, to see what the trade of their sweethearts would be. Looking at an egg in a glass in this fashion was considered a fairly benign and common form of witchcraft, so-called white witchcraft. When they thought they saw a coffin in the glass, their guilt turned to terror.

In February 1692, Betty Parris and Abigail Williams began slipping into trances, blurting nonsensical phrases, cowering in corners, and collapsing in epileptic-like fits. Their bodies were supposedly twisted as if their bones were made out of putty. Reverend Parris invited many doctors to examine the children. No doctor knew what to make of the situation until Doctor William Griggs examined the girls and diagnosed witchcraft.

Reverend Parris asked his congregation to pray and fast, hoping that this would end the witchcraft. They prayed for weeks, but the girls still babbled nonsense and had fits. As more members of the congregation became aware of the problem, the behavior spread to other girls who might also have been experimenting with the occult. Among them were Ann Putnam, Jr., 12, Mary Warren, 20, Mercy Lewis, 19, Mary Walcott, 16, and Elizabeth Hubbard, 17.

The symptoms exhibited have been called "hysteria," but there is confusion about what this term means. In its common usage, it is understood to mean a temporary state of excitement in which the victim loses self-control. However, the term in medicine is far more serious and may include the types of fits observed at the time, as well as temporary loss of hearing, sight, speech, and memory. Symptoms may extend to a choking sensation in the throat, hallucinations, and feelings of being pinched or bitten, even leaving marks on the skin.

In more modern times such fits have been reported. During World War II, British military hospitals reported that seizures in connection with hysteria occurred in only six cases of hysteria out of 161, while during the same time period, the behavior was the most common symptom among hysterics in Delhi, India. Fear of witchcraft rather than its practice seems the most likely cause of the behavior that occurred in Salem.

As Reverend Parris questioned the girls further, they told him Tituba was the witch. Tituba was Reverend Parris's slave, who was from Barbados. While Reverend Parris seems to have been hesitant to believe the doctor's diagnosis, his neighbors were more ready to believe it. On February 25, Mary Sibley, the aunt of Mary Walcott, went to Tituba and asked her to prepare a witch cake—meal mixed with the children's urine, baked in fire, and fed to the Parris's dog. The dog was a "familiar"—a messenger assigned to a witch by the devil. This also was considered white magic, but Reverend Parris was appalled when he found out a month later because he felt the community should go to God, not the devil, even in a good cause.

However, the magic worked—the girls were able to name those afflicting them as Sarah Good and Sarah Osborne. On March 1, 1692, Tituba, Sarah Good, and Sarah Osborne were arrested for practicing witchcraft. Two Salem magistrates who would conduct most of the preliminary examinations, John Hathorne and Jonathan Corwin, questioned the women. John Hathorne asked most of the questions and acted more like a prosecuting attorney than an impartial investigator, as had been the case in past investigations in New England. Hathorne also asked the girls to confront Sarah Good. When they accused her to her face, they immediately were beset by fits, which they said were caused by Good's specter.

Tituba eventually confessed, naming four other witches, Good, Osborne, and two others she did not know. She described the devil as a tall man in a black suit who had a yellow bird, and he carried a book he urged Tituba to sign. There were nine marks in the book, two by Good and Osborne. He promised to give her nice things if she obeyed him, but he also threatened to hurt her if she disobeyed him. Tituba then confessed to trying to kill children while she was in the form of a specter, a ghostly image, a visible disembodied spirit that haunts the mind. Tituba's confession affected the outcome of the witch trials, because she supported the claims of the girls' seeing specters. This made it possible for them to identify witches.

The three women were sent to the Boston jail to await trial, but the magistrates in Salem Village continued to question the afflicted until the names of other witches and the grand wizard were revealed. Two weeks later, Ann Putnam and Abigail Williams named Martha Corey as a witch. Martha Corey was a woman who was respected in the village, and she attended church every Sabbath. She was arrested the day after Abigail Williams pointed out her specter.

Martha Corey's husband, Giles, was called to testify. He said that he found it hard to pray when she was around. He also said he would find her late at night by the hearth kneeling mysteriously. This testimony was accepted as proof that Mrs. Corey was a witch. Mrs. Corey soon joined Tituba, Sarah Good, and Sarah Osborne in the Boston jail. She was the first "gospel woman" to be marked as a witch.

Soon Mary Warren was arrested. Abigail Williams said she had seen Mary sign the devil's book. She said she had also seen her in specter form, and she pinched and hurt her. Abigail and the others also accused John Proctor's wife, Elizabeth. When Proctor came to his wife's defense, he also was arrested. Rebecca Nurse and her sisters Sarah Cloyce and Mary Easty also were arrested. All three were educated, devout Christians. In April 1692, Sarah Good gave birth, and a few weeks later, the baby died. Sarah Osborne also died while in jail. By the end of May 1692, nearly one hundred people had been arrested on charges of witchcraft. Bail was denied and no one yet had been tried by a jury.

Because Massachusetts Colony had just received a new charter from England in May 1692, after eight years without one, no courts were established yet. The new governor, Sir William Phips, realized that the witchcraft trials could not wait until the previously planned date of January 1693. So on May 27, Governor Phips established a special Court of Oyer and Terminer with seven experienced and distinguished judges, headed by William Stoughton, Phips's lieutenant governor.

The court met June 2 and tried one person—Bridget Bishop. She had been charged of using witchcraft in April. She was a woman in her fifties who was twice widowed and married to a third husband. Rumor had it that she had been unfaithful to all three of her husbands. She had been accused with spectral evidence (two women testified that they had seen the devil enter her body), but that alone was not enough. Two laborers who had worked for her had found dolls with pins in them stuffed into holes in the cellar walls in her previous house. This was concrete evidence of the practice of witchcraft and made her conviction relatively easy. She was hanged on June 10, 1692.

However, such concrete evidence did not exist against the other accused witches. Apparently, other types of evidence had proved to be enough to convince the judges. Evidence accepted by the court included self-confession; accusation by others, including other accused witches; being caught in lies; inability to say the Lord's Prayer without error; spectral evidence of the afflicted girls; and marks of the devil on the bodies of the accused.

On June 30, five people were tried, convicted, and condemned to death—Sarah Good, Rebecca Nurse, Susannah Martin, Elizabeth Howe, and Sarah Wildes. On July 19, they were all executed. The morning after, Rebecca Nurse's body was missing. Her family had come and taken her body to have a secret Christian burial for her, although it was against the law to have a Christian burial for a condemned person. The other four bodies were dumped in a shallow grave near the gallows, at a place known as Gallows Hill.

On August 6, the court sat again to consider the cases of six people—John and Elizabeth Proctor, George Burroughs, John Willard, George Jacobs, Sr., and Martha Carrier. All were found guilty and sentenced to death. Elizabeth Proctor's death was delayed because she was pregnant. By the time her baby was born in January 1693, the witch trials were over, so her life was spared.

John Proctor wrote a letter to five area ministers on July 23, on behalf of himself and the other prisoners. He said that the community had condemned them before their trials and asked that the ministers intercede to have the venue of the trials changed or to have the judges changed. Governor Phips was the only one who could make any changes, but Proctor hoped to gain more influence than had been the case with Rebecca Nurse's family, who had sent a petition to the governor as well.

Eight more people were hanged on September 22, 1692, including Martha Corey. Giles Corey, her husband, had been crushed to death just three days earlier for refusing to enter a plea. They laid him down, placed a board over him, and stacked large flat rocks on top of him. They placed the rocks one on top of the other until his rib cage caved in, an agonizing death, taking two days. Although there has been debate on the reasons he chose to die this way, it seems clear that it was done in protest against the court and its proceedings, since none of the accused witches had yet been found not guilty and he was bound to die in any case.

The tide began to turn against the witch hunt, for a number of reasons, including sympathy among the public for some of those condemned, such as Proctor, Corey, and George Burroughs, who was able to recite the Lord's Prayer without error. Also, the afflicted girls began to accuse influential people, including the wife of Increase Mather, the president of Harvard College. He responded by writing *Cases of Conscience*. He warned of the danger of accusing innocent people of witchcraft, especially those in good standing in the church.

A third reason was that the court was not accomplishing its purpose, which was to clear the jails. The more the court sat, the more crowded the jails became and the greater the disturbances in the community. The afflicted girls had not gotten better, but worse. In the nearby town of Andover, where witchcraft accusations were spreading fast, an accused man of means sent friends around town to inquire who his accusers were so that he could sue them for defamation of character. Shortly, accusations were halted.

The witch trial era lasted less than a year. The first arrests were made in March 1692 and the final hanging day was September 22, 1692. Jurors and magistrates apologized. Restitution was made to the victims' families, and a Day of Fasting and Remembrance was instituted. Many of the girls, such as Ann Putnam, later admitted that no evil hand had touched them. The girls were enmeshed in the beliefs of the community and became convinced that evil forces had bewitched them.

To understand the issues of the Salem witch trials in that time frame, it is important to place them into a broader historical context. As early as the fifth century, Saint Augustine saw sorcery and white magic as being dependent on the help of the devil. In the mid-thirteenth century, Saint Thomas Aquinas agreed with Saint Augustine. At this time, the Inquisition, composed mainly of members of the newly formed Dominican order, was formed to deal with heresy. The Dominicans were the first to use torture to gain confessions, and by the late fourteenth century, this policy became the norm in secular courts as well.

In 1486, Henirich Kramer and Jacob Sprenger published *Malleus Maleficarum*, or *The Witches' Hammer*. They had been involved for over five years in witchcraft trials that resulted in nearly fifty executions. *The Witches' Hammer* was written in the form of a handbook and was convenient for use by judges. It remained an important work for over 200 years.

Statistics vary, but the pace of prosecutions picked up in the last three-quarters of the fifteenth century and then skyrocketed from the last half of the sixteenth through the seventeenth centuries, reaching a peak in the last half of the seventeenth century. Between 1365 and 1428, there were 84 verified prosecutions, increasing to 354 between 1428 and 1500. In Europe, figures range as high as 10,000 executions for witchcraft, with 900 in the city of Bamburg and 5,000 in the province of Alsace, 368 in Trier, 274 in Eichstatt, and 390 in Ellwangen. The English and Swiss were more restrained, as were the American colonies. There were fewer than fifty executions in the American colonies during the seventeenth century, including those in Salem. The parallels between the Salem witch trials and more modern examples such as the McCarthy hearings of the 1950s have also been studied.

In 1992, the town of Salem observed the tercentenary of the Salem witch trials. Among the many events in Salem that year, a memorial was dedicated and Professor Joseph Flibbert of Salem State College organized a conference that brought scholars to Salem from around the world to discuss the trials and other topics related to witchcraft. On September 20, 1992, the First Church in Salem readmitted Giles Corey and Rebecca Nurse to church membership.

INTERPRETIVE ESSAY
Frederick M. Stowell

At the end of the twentieth century, American society has become jaded by stories of violence and the persistent images of this violence on television and in the media. Whether those images are generated by war, social unrest, or natural disaster, they have become commonplace as Americans expect more realism and graphic details in the reporting of current events. In this environment of information overload, the Salem witchcraft trials of 1692 still hold the interest of the general public and generate analysis by social scientists, historians, and researchers. The events that occurred more than 300 years ago and affected a relatively small number of people have made Salem synonymous with witch hunts and mass hysteria. The significance of the trials in Salem, Massachusetts, is not earth shaking but subtle. It did not have the effect on society of the Declaration of Independence or the War of 1812, yet it is still used as a benchmark by which to judge other occurrences of group hysteria. This traditional interpretation of a Massachusetts community in turmoil, generated over a century ago, has become the popular image of the colonial witch hunt craze.

The significance of the Salem witchcraft trials, however, is more than just the traditional interpretation of group hysteria. The trials are an opportunity to view the dynamics of a primitive frontier culture, established in a hostile environment, clinging to its European beliefs, and restricted by its dogmatic religious beliefs. While group hysteria played a part in the accusations of witchcraft and the resulting trials, the actual causes of the witch craze were rooted in the frontier society of the colony and its European traditions. Political instability, economic uncertainty and conflict, and the threat of war with the local Native American nations were clear and present concerns to the residents of Salem. Add to this the ingrained fear of a demonic presence, and the male dominant view that women were a threat to the church, the government, and the society, and it becomes apparent how an atmosphere of hysteria could develop and grow.

In order to understand fully the significance of the 1692 Salem witchcraft trials, it is necessary to understand the variety of historical interpretations and the influence of the period during which the interpretations

were written. The earliest writings on the trials occurred shortly after
the trials ended in 1692. The Reverend Cotton Mather, a member of the
Puritan hierarchy in Massachusetts, recorded the events leading up to
the trials and the accusations and testimonies of the trials in an attempt
to justify the verdicts. His own position was that the trials were justified
and carried out within the laws of the colony and Christianity. His view
was different from that of his father, Increase Mather, who preached
moderation and rationality. A counterpoint to Cotton Mather's writings
were those of Robert Calef, a Boston merchant who witnessed the trials
and executions. In his book *More Wonders of the Invisible World* (1701),
Calef suggests that the evil could be found not in the witchcraft but in
the very trials themselves. In his view, the witch hunts and trials were
"bigoted zeal" directed toward "virtuous and religious people."

The traditional view that attempted to fix blame for the trials developed from the writings of Charles Upham in 1867. *Salem Witchcraft*,
Upham's two-volume interpretation of the original trial transcripts, attempted to focus blame on the "afflicted" girls as the leaders of a larger
conspiracy against the accused witches. His contention became the popular cultural view that would influence the teaching of the event in
American public schools for the next hundred odd years.

In 1953, Perry Miller delved into the meaning of being a Puritan and
how that faith affected the lives of the colonists and laid the basis for
the trials. This was an important connection for writers attempting to
fully understand the reasons for the witch craze in New England and
specifically Salem. Miller focused on the Puritan covenant or relationship
they believed they had with God. As the Puritans worked to serve God
and establish a community to do his will on earth, they truly believed
that seeking out witches and destroying them was part of that covenant.
When they realized that something had gone wrong with the trials, the
foundation of this relationship with God came into question. Miller's
interpretation of this relationship and the resulting confusion of belief
added to an increased understanding of the events.

By the late 1960s other researchers began to take different approaches
to the cause of the witch craze. Chadwick Hansen in *Witchcraft at Salem*
(1969) argued that witchcraft really did exist in Salem as well as other
parts of New England. Folk magic was widely used by the early colonists, and the activities of the first afflicted girls in Salem were not out of
the ordinary. Since the community believed in the power of magic and

some of the accused were admitted witches, then witchcraft must have existed. According to Hanson, the trials were justified in that context.

Other views about the cause of the craze include a virus among the afflicted, the dominance of men and the low position of women in the society, the economic struggle between the rural and commercial centers of Salem Village and Salem Town, the demographics of the affected regions, and the power struggle within the community. All of these have developed since the 1960s as more researchers have attempted to go beyond the trials and look at the complex issues of the community. The idea that a virus was the cause was posited in 1976 and has largely been discredited. The feminist approach, which Carol Karlsen first developed in *Devil in the Shape of a Woman* (1987), attempted to analyze the trial and accusations in light of late-twentieth-century concepts about the treatment of women. From this point of view, the author expands the descriptions of the accused witches from disagreeable old hags to women who were guilty because they were different. She states that gender issues merged with religious issues and that these were seen to be transgressions against God. Displays of anger, temper, and discontent with the church all were seen as signs of an alliance with the devil. Additionally, women who practiced healing and midwifery, assisting in the birth process, were seen as threats to the developing male medical profession. Although midwifery was not a sign of demonic involvement, it was enough to bring suspicion upon the accused.

Three researchers, John Demos, Paul Boyer, and Stephen Nissenbaum, attempted to go outside the actual trial and look at the social environment of the community. Through their research, the full picture of a community in turmoil was developed. Taken together, their works explain why certain people became accusers and others became victims. The authors paint a picture of old animosities, lawsuits, and rivalries. It is through the view of these authors that a more detailed perspective of the community and the trials develops.

Even the heritage of Tituba, the Indian slave of Samuel Parris, has been traced as far back as her documented origin in the Caribbean. Details of plantation life in the islands that influenced Tituba and ultimately Salem have been reconstructed through diligent research.

The events of 1692 in Salem, Massachusetts, have provided Americans with an example of a community gripped by group hysteria. This traditional and very general view was originally created in the writing of Charles Upham in 1867 and then incorporated into the massive *History of the United States* (1883–85) by George Bancroft. From there it found its way into the history texts of American public schools and into American popular culture. This image of young girls writhing in pain, afflicted by unknown demons, and stern-faced Puritan men in austere black clothing sitting in judgment of haggard old women, made its way into American culture in art, in literature, and on stage. Instilled into the collective memory of Americans, the Salem trials have become a benchmark for any similar event where unfounded accusations lead to the suffering of innocent victims. It has provided a perfect example of people being guilty until proven innocent. The playwright Arthur Miller used it for the theme of his play *The Crucible* (1953), which was also an analogy for the anticommunist movement of the early 1950s. The image of the "witch hunt" has been used to refer to this anticommunist Red Scare of both the post–World War I years and the McCarthyism of the early 1950s. In the former event, Americans were accused of association with the communist party and in some cases, deported. During the latter, those accused of communist ties were hounded out of positions of authority in the government or jobs in the private sector. McCarthyism, named for the U.S. senator who led the anticommunist movement, has come to mean publicly accusing a person without evidence of guilt, or guilt by association.

Additionally, the Salem trials have provided an intimate view of the much greater witch craze that had gripped Europe during the fifteenth and seventeenth centuries. The accusations of 150 people and the deaths of twenty accused witches in Salem was much more personal than the deaths of an estimated two hundred thousand people in Europe. The accused, the accusers, and the magistrates in Salem are known by name, and their words reverberate from the trial transcripts. The examinations by William Stoughton, chief justice of the Court of Oyer and Terminer, the accusations of Ann Putnam, the denials of Mary Easty, and even the silence of Giles Corey, all provide a personal view of the participants. The events of Salem also show the influence of the European-based superstitions on the colonists. The actions of the first accusers, Betty Parris, Abigail Williams, and Ann Putnam, Jr., were based on European superstition and not the supposed voodoo of Tituba, Samuel Parris's Caribbean Indian slave. The practice of fortune-telling through the reading of eggs dropped in a glass was part of English folklore and not unusual in the Puritan communities of North America. So the girls were simply following an established magical practice that had migrated with the Puritans from England.

If the popular view of Salem has been one of mass hysteria, the reality of the situation was somewhat different. The events of Salem can be viewed as the result of an unstable environment, composed of political uncertainty, threats of war, and the fear of change, that generated an atmosphere of fear within the community. That fear found its focal point in the witch hunts and trials.

At the beginning of the Salem witch craze, the Massachusetts colony was without a charter, a governor, or a legally recognized government. The original charter, issued in 1630, had been revoked by King Charles II in 1684 in an attempt to increase English control over the profitable American colonies. With the ascension of James II, brother of King Charles II, to the throne, Massachusetts became part of the Dominion of New England, made up of New York, New Jersey, New Hampshire, Connecticut, Plymouth, and part of Maine. In 1686 King James II appointed Sir Edmund Andros to govern the new dominion. Andros began to govern with a heavy hand, imposing taxes without legislative approval, challenging all land titles, and allowing religious dissent in the formerly Puritan stronghold of Massachusetts. This threat of change caused a fear within the Puritan leadership as they saw their control slipping away. With the Glorious Revolution in England and Parliament's overthrow of James II in 1689, the colonists who hoped for a return to the status quo ousted Andros. The interim government, called the Council of Safety and made up of Boston merchants and magistrates, would lead the colony until the arrival of the new governor and charter in 1692, four months after the start of the witch hunt. In this environment of political instability, the accusations and arrests of witches took place in a vacuum lacking a legal framework. Without the guidance and justification of law, the magistrates found the necessary validation for their actions in the word of God.

Throughout the colony, fear of impending war with the local Native American Nations was also spreading. King Philip's War of 1675–76, massacres at Lancaster in 1676, and the Native American involvement in King William's War in 1688 were all part of recent memory. Rumors were rampant in 1692 that the Native Americans were preparing to mount another assault on the colonists. In addition, early settlers believed that there was a Satanic presence that permeated Native American life. This belief even spilled over into the accusation of Captain John Alden as a witch. He became suspect of witchcraft through his association with the Native Americans. Prior to the trials he had worked to create a better relationship between the colonists and the Native Americans. Add to this the belief that the Native Americans were in league with the devil, and there is little wonder that the residents of Salem were on edge.

Fear was also part of the Puritan faith. Fear of the devil was instilled through the sermons of the church leaders and parish preachers. In Boston, the sermons of Cotton Mather were filled with warnings of the power of the devil and the existence of evil in the world, an evil that was a direct threat to the Puritan vision of a holy utopia in the new world. The Salem preacher, the Reverend Samuel Parris, invoked the threat of the devil in his sermons to explain the turmoil within his own parish prior to the witch hunts. And it was not difficult to maintain this fear of evil: The belief in the devil and witchcraft was real for the European settlers. Based on biblical passages, Puritans were certain that the devil walked the earth and, in particular, Massachusetts. Worse yet, they believed that women, weak and easily coerced, could be seduced by the devil. According to Puritan beliefs women were unable to resist the devil and therefore subject to the ways of witchcraft. Finding its roots in the Bible, this belief dated from the telling of the story of Eve, the Snake and the Garden of Eden. This belief explains the fact that the majority of the accused and convicted witches in Salem, in the rest of the colonies, and in Europe were women.

Finally, the fear of change infected the participants. The arrival of Governor William Phips and the new charter in May 1692 signaled that the Puritans had lost local political control. Not only were the Puritan leaders concerned over the loss of political power but they also worried about the threat posed by women. The male-dominated Puritan society was afraid of any woman who was different, strong-willed, questioning of authority, even argumentative. Anne Hutchinson, who had questioned the authority of the Puritan Church in Massachusetts, had been excommunicated and exiled to Rhode Island in 1638. This would be an omen for the deadly events of 1692. The male leadership also feared the change that was apparent in the commercial success that Salem Town was undergoing while the members of the rural Salem Village languished in an economic backwater. Finally, the Puritans were grasped by fear that was caused by the loss of control as non-Puritans migrated to the colony and began to demand equal authority and rights. This loss of control began with the heavy-handed authority of Governor Sir Edmund Andros. He attempted to established the presence of the Anglican Church in Boston, the seat of Puritanism, and to legislate religious tolerance in the colony. His actions would be an omen for the change that would come. All of this fear added to the desire to find a reason why God had apparently forsaken his people and allowed the devil to reign in Massachusetts.

The events of 1692 also provide the validation for the theory of separation of church and state. The Massachusetts colony has been referred to as a theocracy, a governmental form where the state religion provides the leadership for the government. This was not quite true of Massachusetts. Elected officials did not have to be members of the clergy. However, the right to vote was restricted to male members of the Puritan Church, and the laws were filled with scriptural references to justify this arrangement. Scripture validated not only male dominance and the divine right of the Puritans, as they saw it, but also the evil incarnate in women.

This merging of law and scripture allowed for the most flagrant violation of individual rights during the Salem witchcraft trials, the use of spectral evidence in the accusation of the afflicted. Spectral evidence, the concept that the afflicted had been visited by an image of the accused, was the basis for all of the guilty judgments save those accused persons who admitted their guilt. Founded in English law, it allowed for the unsubstantiated claim of one individual against another without the opportunity for the victim to prove otherwise. Because witchcraft was considered a capital offense, the accused were denied the right to legal counsel. As one author put it, the accused were required to "defend against the indefensible." The judges sincerely believed that the trials were held in an enlightened and rational manner, using scientific principles of law and humane behavior. Besides the spectral evidence, the use of physical marks, called the devil's mark, on the bodies of the accused, were used to prove guilt. Finally, the existence of the witches teat, a third nipple allegedly used to suckle the witch's "familiar," was certain evidence that the accused was part of the devil's coven. Familiars were usually cats, dogs, or even toads who helped the witch in her work with the devil. Accused witches were forced to submit to humiliating searches by female matrons as the magistrates sought solid evidence. In late May 1692, physical searches were made of six of the accused. Bridget Bishop, Rebecca Nurse, and Elizabeth Proctor were all found to have marks. The other three, Susannah Martin, Sarah Good, and Alice Parker, were free of blemishes. In a second search later in the day, the marks on Bishop and Proctor had disappeared. This remarkable discovery was seen as further proof that the women were witches. Of these six women, only Elizabeth Proctor would escape execution, and then only because she was pregnant.

One major influence on the trials was the Puritan concept of redemption through repentance. Sinners who asked forgiveness and admitted their failings were perceived as able to return to God's grace. Individuals who stood by their faith and denied any failings were seen as denying the grace of God. During the witchcraft trials, the accused who admitted their guilt were spared execution. Some even became witnesses against other accused witches, including their wives and husbands. Those who denied their guilt, as did Rebecca Nurse, were found guilty and punished. In the case of Giles Corey, who refused to plead innocent or guilty, English law and not Puritan beliefs sealed his fate. Corey was crushed to death from the weight of rocks placed upon his chest. The rocks that were intended to force a plea from him resulted only in his silent death.

Finally, and perhaps most importantly, the events of Salem provided a documented example of community life and relations in colonial America. Initially this view was limited to the analysis of the trial documents, which illustrated the activities of the legal system and the Puritan views on witchcraft. With the passing of time, Salem became the laboratory for social scientists who investigated other aspects of community life in search of causes for the witch craze. The influence of Puritan belief, the effects of sermons, and the influence of the clergy on the lives of people were studied. In particular, the sermons and writings of Cotton Mather and Samuel Parris were analyzed. Mather and Parris have both been held responsible for helping to create the atmosphere of fear that permeated Massachusetts. The responses of Robert Calef and John Hale provided the opposing view of clergy who questioned the trials and the guilt of the accused. The writings of each of the clergy provided an intimate view of the dominance of religion in local life.

Local politics, which illustrated the conflict between the agricultural Salem Village and the commercial Salem Town, became the focus of interest in the 1960s as researchers sought further causes for the craze. The people of Salem Village felt that they were losing control and were being overshadowed by the economically successful Salem Town. Researchers found that a pattern of accusations of witches correlated with economic troubles. Also apparent were the local power struggles between groups within the village who supported or disliked the Reverend Samuel Parris. Documents describing lawsuits, land claims, and debts created a network that also followed the network of accusers, accused, witnesses, and supporters. Researchers have prepared maps defining the residence of each participant in the witch craze and genealogical charts showing the family relationships. Of the twenty-two men accused, eleven were closely related to the accused women. Eight other men were accused through more casual association with the women. The relative position of people in Massachusetts society also became apparent. At first the list of the accused included only the poor and widowed. As the spring of 1692 turned into summer, the list began to include members of the economic elite whose piety and status was firmly established. Rebecca Nurse, wife of a respected land owner, was accused and executed despite her piety and reputation within the community. George Burroughs, the former Salem Village minister, also became a victim of the trials. When this pattern started to develop, it became apparent that the accusers could no longer be believed and something had to be done. When Governor William Phips's wife was accused, he called a halt to the proceedings, disbanded the Court of Oyer and Terminer, ceased all executions, and finally pardoned those still in jail.

The Salem witch craze and the ensuing trials may have had neither the devastating effect on people that the European witch hunts did nor a direct effect on the overall social, economic, political, legal, or international climate in colonial America. However, the trials did provide a traditional example for group hysteria that found its way into the American self-image. Beyond that, the trials have continued to provide an intimate and detailed view of early colonial America and the difficulties of living on the frontier far from the accepted way of life.

SELECTED BIBLIOGRAPHY

Boyer, Paul, and Nissenbaum, Stephen. *Salem Possessed: The Social Origins of Witchcraft*. Cambridge, MA: Harvard University Press, 1974. An excellent source for understanding the social background of the witch craze and trials.

———. *The Salem Witchcraft Papers: Verbatim Transcripts of the Legal Documents of the Salem Witchcraft Outbreak of 1692*. New York: Da Capo, 1977. The currently accepted source for the official trial transcripts.

Breslaw, Elaine G. *Tituba, Reluctant Witch of Salem—Devilish Indians and Puritan Fantasies*. New York: New York University Press, 1996. A well-researched book on the origins of the slave Tituba and an interpretation of her part in the witch craze and trials.

Demos, John P. *Entertaining Satan: Witchcraft and the Culture of Early New England*. New York: Oxford University Press, 1982. A view of witchcraft in seventeenth-century New England from the historical, sociological, psychological, and biographical perspectives.

Drake, Samuel, G., comp. *The Witchcraft Delusion in New England. . . .* New York: B. Franklin, 1970. This volume includes Robert Calef, *More Wonders of the*

Invisible World, an early (1701) account of the Salem Witch trials by one who considered them to be evil.

Hall, David D., ed. *Puritanism in Seventeenth Century Massachusetts.* New York: Holt Rinehart and Winston, 1968. A collection of essays by various authors on Puritan beliefs in Massachusetts.

Hansen, Chadwick. *Witchcraft at Salem.* New York: George Braziller, 1969. Takes the view that witchcraft did exist in Salem and that the hysteria was a real affliction for the accusers.

Hill, Frances. *A Delusion of Satan: The Full Story of the Salem Witch Trials.* New York: Da Capo, 1997. A recent retelling of the story that is very subjective but does not break any new ground or provide a substantially different interpretation.

Karlsen, Carol F. *The Devil in the Shape of a Woman.* New York: W. W. Norton, 1987. Provides a feminist view of the trials emphasizing a male dominant society and its effect on the outcome of the trials.

Klaits, Joseph. *Servants of Satan: The Age of the Witch Hunts.* Bloomington: Indiana University Press, 1985. A good source for the broader historical context of the Salem witch trials.

Mappen, Marc, ed. *Witches and Historians: Interpretations of Salem.* Huntington, CA: Robert E. Krieger, 1980. A series of essays by various historians comparing the shifting interpretations of the causes of the Salem witch trials.

Marshall, Richard. *Witchcraft: The History and Mythology.* New York: Crescent Books, 1995. An illustrated volume on the history of witchcraft to the present that includes a chapter on the Salem trial.

Miller, Arthur. *The Crucible, a Play in Four Acts.* New York: Viking, 1953. The celebrated stageplay about the Salem witch trials that many saw as a commentary on contemporary McCarthyism and its "witch" hunts.

Miller, Perry. *The New England Mind: From Colony to Province.* Cambridge, MA: Harvard University Press, 1953. An explanation of the Puritan intellectual and social world of the seventeenth century.

Upham, Charles W. *Salem Witchcraft.* New York: Frederick Ungar, 1959. Originally published in 1867, this is the traditional view of the Salem event from the group hysteria standpoint.

Appendix A

Glossary

Baltimore, Lord [Charles Calvert] (1637–1715). Charles Calvert, the third Lord Baltimore, was the Catholic proprietor of Maryland from 1675 to 1715, although much of his political power was removed after the Glorious Revolution. He was the grandson of George Calvert, the first Lord Baltimore, to whom King Charles I granted the territory in the 1630s.

Charles II (1630–1685). King of England (1660–1685) after the end of the English Civil War (1649–1660). He worked to reunify England after the civil war, fought trade wars with the Dutch, and battled with Parliament over questions of religious toleration.

Charles IX (1550–1574). Short-lived, weak-minded King of France (1560–1574), Charles IX was on the throne when Admiral Gaspard de Coligny sent a Huguenot expedition to establish a colony in Florida.

Council of Trade and Plantations. Established by King Charles II in 1674 to handle colonial matters, but replaced by the Board of Trade and Plantations, a parliamentary committee, after the Glorious Revolution.

Declaration of Indulgence (1687). Issued by King James II of England, this granted Catholics freedom from penalties to which they had been liable if they practiced their religion. This and subsequent pro-Catholic actions of the king led to the Glorious Revolution.

Ferdinand II (1452–1516) and *Isabella I* (1451–1504). King and queen of

Spain following the union of the kingdoms of Castile and Aragon in 1469. They sponsored Columbus's first three voyages, drove Jews who would not convert to Catholicism from Spain, and finished the *reconquista*, the process of expelling Muslims, or Moors, from Spain.

Hakluyt, Richard (1552–1616). An English geographer and chronicler, Hakluyt published between 1582 and 1600 a number of important accounts of voyages to America and helped popularize the notion of English imperial expansion. Sometimes he is referred to as Richard Hakluyt the Younger to distinguish him from his cousin, Richard Hakluyt the Elder, who raised him and inspired his love of geography.

Henry VII (1457–1509). King of England (1485–1509) during the earliest voyages of exploration, Henry did much to unify England under his rule and to broaden its commercial outlook and contacts.

Huguenots. This is the name applied to French Protestants, who lost their civil and religious freedom (and in some cases, their lives) in 1685 when Louis XIV issued a decree known as the Edict of Nantes. Many immigrated to the North American colonies, following a practice that had begun in the 1560s.

James I (1566–1625). King of England (1603–1625), and as James VI, King of Scotland (1567–1625). James was the monarch for whom the settlement of Jamestown was named, and in his name, other settlements were founded. He achieved popularity at the end of his reign when he requested that Parliament declare war on Spain after the Spanish court rejected a marriage offer between his son Charles and the daughter of the Spanish king.

James II (1633–1701). King of England (1685–1688) and brother of Charles II. James's fondness for Catholicism led to the Glorious Revolution in 1688 and his subsequent exile in France.

King William's War (1689–1697). The first of several colonial wars fought between the French and English between 1689 and 1763. Most of the fighting took place in the area near the St. Lawrence River, although at one point attacked the northern border of New Hampshire. The war ended with the Treaty of Ryswick (1697), which restored matters to their pre-war state.

Mary II (1662–1694). Queen of England (1689–1694) in conjunction with her husband, William III. The daughter of James II, she deferred to William on most state matters and died of smallpox at a young age, leaving no children.

Mather, Increase (1639–1723). One of the most prominent Puritan clergymen, Mather was president of Harvard in the 1680s and became involved in the politics surrounding the Glorious Revolution as Massachusetts's agent in London from 1688 to 1692. His somewhat belated objection to the conduct of the Salem witch trials helped bring an end to that event. He was the father of Cotton Mather, an equally important Puritan clergyman between the 1690s and the 1720s.

McCarthy hearings (1950–1954). Senator Joseph McCarthy (Rep., WI) made a name for himself in the Cold War era through his leadership of an anticommunist crusade that many critics called a "witch hunt." Some of the more celebrated "witches" were "hunted" by means of congressional hearings.

Mutiny Act (1689). A consequence of the Glorious Revolution, this act of Parliament limited the size of the military and authorized the use of the court-martial to enforce military justice. The act had to be renewed annually, thus helping to guarantee frequent sessions of Parliament.

Navigation Act (1651). Part of English imperial trade policy, sometimes referred to as mercantilism. This act of Parliament barred foreign ships from trading with English colonies and prohibited imports that did not arrive in England on either English ships or those of the country of origin. Certain "enumerated" colonial products, like tobacco, could be sent only to English ports. This and other navigation acts were designed to limit the ability of the Dutch and other European rivals to trade with the American colonies.

Opechancanough (d. 1644). The son of Powhatan, Opechancanough took his father's place as head of the Powhatan federation in 1618 and fought various battles with the Virginia colonists before his capture and murder in 1644.

Pocahontas (1595–1617). The daughter of Powhatan, Pocahontas reputedly saved the life of John Smith, leader of the Jamestown Colony, in 1608 after her father had captured him. After her conversion to Christianity, she married colonist John Rolfe in 1614 and died in England in 1617.

Powhatan (1550–1618). Also known as Wahunsunacock, he was chief of the Powhatan federation when the first settlers came to Virginia. A strong leader, Powhatan became more friendly and tolerant of the colonists after the marriage of his daughter Pocahontas to John Rolfe.

Spanish Armada. The name given to a fleet of 130 ships sent to participate in an invasion of England in 1588. In a major naval battle in the English Channel in late July and early August, England's more maneuverable ships and better guns led to the rout of the Spanish fleet. The defeat of the armada was a major boost to England's imperial ambitions and a severe blow to Spanish international prestige.

Toleration Act (1688). During the Glorious Revolution, Parliament approved this measure, which allowed dissenting Protestants freedom from attending Church of England services and the right to attend their own church. The act granted other rights to Protestant dissenters and their ministers, but Roman Catholics were not covered under its provisions.

William III (1650–1702). A native of the Netherlands, he became King of England (1689–1702) as a result of his marriage to Mary, the oldest child of James II, and the Glorious Revolution, which drove his father-in-law from power. As king, he was staunchly Protestant and fought a lengthy war against the French that distracted him from concern about the English colonies in North America.

Williams, Roger (c. 1603–1683). An English minister who arrived in New England in 1630 and became an opponent of the Puritan hierarchy. He founded the colony of Rhode Island as a haven of religious toleration and enjoyed amiable relations with the Indians.

Appendix B

Timeline

c. 40,000 B.C.E.	First people arrive in North America from Asia
c. 5000 B.C.E.	Crop cultivation begins in Mexico and spreads throughout North America
c. 800	Norse colonies established in Iceland
c. 1000	Leif Eriksson leads voyage to east coast of Canada
1325	Founding of Aztec capital, Tenochtitian
1492	First voyage of Christopher Columbus
1493	First permanent Spanish settlement in New World
1497	John Cabot's first voyage to eastern coast of Canada
1508–11	Decimation of Native population of West Indies by disease and warfare
1513	Juan Ponce de León arrives in and names Florida
1517	Spanish begin bringing African slaves to South and Central America
1519	Hernan Cortés begins conquest of Aztec society in Mexico
1527–28	Pánfilo de Narváez expedition to Gulf Coast region

1539–42	Hernando de Soto expedition to Gulf Coast region
1540–42	Coronado's expedition to present-day southwestern United States
1561	Tristán de Luna expedition attempts to settle near Pensacola
1564	Laudonnière establishes French colony near Atlantic Coast of Florida
1565	Spanish establish colony of St. Augustine, Florida
1584	First English attempt to plant a colony in North America
1588	Defeat of the Spanish Armada
1607	English establish first permanent colony at Jamestown
1609	Henry Hudson sails up Hudson River; claims area for Dutch
1612	Powhatan teach English in Virginia to cultivate tobacco
1614	Pocahontas and John Rolfe marry
1616–17	Smallpox epidemic kills many New England Indians
1619	First Africans brought to Virginia as slaves
1620	Pilgrims establish colony at Plymouth, Massachusetts
1624	First permanent Dutch colony established at New Netherland
1630	Puritan colony established in Massachusetts under John Winthrop
1634	Lord Baltimore establishes Catholic colony of Maryland
1636	Roger Williams establishes colony of Rhode Island
1637	Pequot War in New England
1644	Final significant Indian uprising in Virginia
1651	Parliament approves first of several Navigation Acts
1658	Esopus rebellion against Dutch in New Netherland
1664	English force Dutch surrender of New Netherland
1675–76	King Philip's War in New England
1676	Bacon's Rebellion in Virginia

1681	William Penn given land grant and charter to established Pennsylvania
1688–89	Glorious Revolution in England
1691	Leisler's Rebellion defeated in New York
1692	Salem witch trials in Massachusetts

Index

About the Editors
and Contributors

BLAKE BEATTIE received his Ph.D. from the University of Toronto in 1992 and has taught at the University of Louisville since 1994. His principal field of interest is the later medieval Mediterranean world. He has published on medieval Italian urban society and on court preaching at fourteenth-century Avignon.

THOMAS CLARKIN received his doctorate in U.S. history from the University of Texas at Austin in 1998. He has completed a manuscript on federal Indian policy during the Kennedy and Johnson administrations. He currently teaches at San Antonio College and resides in the Texas Hill Country.

JOHN E. FINDLING is professor of history at Indiana University Southeast. He earned his Ph.D. at the University of Texas and has pursued a research interest in world's fairs for nearly twenty years. He is the author of *Chicago's Great World's Fairs* (1995), and with Robert W. Rydell and Kimberly D. Pelle, the co-author of *Fair America* (2000). With Frank W. Thackeray, he has edited *Statesmen Who Changed the World* (1993) and the other volumes in the *Events that Changed the World* and *Events that Changed America* series.

ANDREW FRANK teaches colonial and Native American history at California State University, Los Angeles. He is the author of *The Routledge*

Historical Atlas of the American South (1996) and *The Birth of Black America: The Age of Discovery and the Slave Trade* (1999). His current project explores intermarriage between Indians and Europeans in the colonial era.

RICK KENNEDY is professor of history at Point Loma Nazarene University in San Diego. He received his Ph.D. from the University of California at Santa Barbara. He wrote the introduction for and edited the Colonial Society of Massachusetts volume *Aristotelian and Cartesian Logic at Harvard* (1995).

THOMAS A. MACKEY is an associate professor and chair of the history department at the University of Louisville. He divides his time between Louisville, Kentucky, and Long Island, New York. He completed his undergraduate studies at Beloit College and his doctoral work at Rice University. Constitutional, legal, and political issues are his specialties.

KATHLEEN PERDISATT graduated with distinction from Point Loma Nazarene University in San Diego in 1999. She is pursuing a career in education.

STEVEN E. SIRY is associate professor of history at Baldwin-Wallace College. He received his Ph.D. from the University of Cincinnati. His publications include articles in the *Journal of the Early Republic, Locus, Statesmen Who Changed the World* (1993), *Events That Changed America in the Nineteenth Century* (1997), and *Events That Changed America in the Eighteenth Century* (1998).

FREDERICK M. STOWELL holds a Master's degree in military history and studies. He is an adjunct instructor at Tulsa Community College and Langston University, teaching courses in history and philosophy. He has presented papers at the Mid-America Conference on History and is a contract writer for the Oklahoma State University Fire Protection publications.

P. D. SWINEY is assistant professor of American history and African-American history at Tulsa Community College, where she has taught for ten years. Her undergraduate degree is from St. Mary's of Notre Dame and her M.A. is from Oklahoma State University in Stillwater. She has a special interest in the Knights of Labor and Alexander Hamilton.

FRANK W. THACKERAY is professor of history at Indiana University Southeast. He received his Ph.D. from Temple University. He is the author of *Antecedents of Revolution: Alexander I and the Polish Congress Kingdom* (1980) as well as articles on Russian-Polish relations in the nineteenth century and Polish-American relations in the twentieth century. With John E. Findling, he edited *Statesmen Who Changed the World* (1993) and the other volumes in the *Events That Changed the World* and *Events that Changed America* series. He is a former Fulbright scholar in Poland.

JULIA A. WOODS is a Ph.D. candidate in history at the University of Texas at Austin. She has an M.A. in history from the University of Texas and a J.D. from the University of North Carolina at Chapel Hill Law School. She is currently researching her dissertation, tentatively titled, "The Bench and Bar of Travis County, Texas, 1835–1880."